100 Ideas for
Secondary Teachers

Engaging Learners

Other titles in the 100 Ideas for Secondary Teachers series

100 Ideas for Secondary Teachers

Engaging Learners

Jon Tait

B L O O M S B U R Y

LONDON · OXFORD · NEW YORK · NEW DELHI · SYDNEY

Bloomsbury Education
An imprint of Bloomsbury Publishing Plc

50 Bedford Square　　　　1385 Broadway
London　　　　　　　　　New York
WC1B 3DP　　　　　　　　NY 10018
UK　　　　　　　　　　　　USA

www.bloomsbury.com

Bloomsbury is a registered trade mark of Bloomsbury Publishing Plc

First published in Great Britain 2017

A catalogue record for this book is available from the British Library.
Library of Congress Cataloguing-in-Publication data has been applied for.

ISBN:
PB 9781472945327
ePub 9781472945334
ePDF 9781472945341

2 4 6 8 10 9 7 5 3 1

Typeset by Newgen Knowledge Works (P) Ltd., Chennai, India
Printed and bound in the UK by CPI Group (UK) Ltd, Croydon CR0 4YY

This book is produced using paper that is made from wood grown in managed, sustainable forests. It is natural, renewable and recyclable. The logging and manufacturing processes conform to the environmental regulations of the country of origin.

To find out more about our authors and books visit www.bloomsbury.com. Here you will find extracts, author interviews, details of forthcoming events and the option to sign up for our newsletters.

This book is dedicated to my amazing wife, Tracy. If Tracy's personal battle in 2014 taught us anything as a family, it's that a positive mindset can beat almost anything. It's all about strength of mind and character. The kids and I will always be indebted to her for showing us what you can achieve with a smile on your face. What got us through was the thought that 'It might be stormy now, but it never rains forever.'

Without a shadow of a doubt, she has become our true hero. x

Contents

Acknowledgements

Firstly I need to thank the one person who has enabled me to stand on the platform I stand on today, my mam...

On A level results day, a little over 20 years ago, I was one of those students, one of the ones trying to slip into the background, putting on a brave face that told the world that my results didn't matter... but they did. My results effectively ruined my plans of moving on to university and taking up a place on my preferred course. For the first time in my life I felt like I had nowhere to go – a homeless academic. My disappointing results had meant that I'd missed the boat – and to make it worse, all my friends were on that boat.

On the way home from college, with my results hidden away from the world in my pocket, I made the decision to go back to college again in the autumn to resit my A levels. My aim was to be able to jump on that boat the next time it was to set sail. Returning home that afternoon, I informed my mam of my results, my feelings and my revised plans for the forthcoming autumn – I wouldn't be spreading my wings as planned.

In the weeks that followed, my mam single-handedly changed my focus and direction. Why waste a year of my life resitting exam results when I could be out there making it happen for myself? The support that I was shown in those few weeks, when I needed it most, has certainly defined my life to date. I was driven to universities across the country to look around, along with trawling through newspapers and calling universities for 'clearing places'. In the end, the course and university I chose, and was accepted at, were just right for me. It was the perfect boat, ready to set sail on the most incredible journey.

With hard work and a desire from that day onwards to be the best that I could be, I managed to create my own passport to life. I'm now a deputy head teacher, helping other young people try to realise their dreams. When I reflect, it is clear that when I needed that home support the most, it was there, and it has shaped who I am today. Support from your parents or loved ones is crucial when making big decisions. Be open, be honest and seek advice from the people who know you best. Even though I thought I knew the direction that I was going to travel, I would have never travelled the journey I have without the support that I received that day. Thanks, Mam x

Secondly I would like to acknowledge and thank all of the amazing and inspirational colleagues that I have had the privilege of working with, watching and learning from over the years. The ideas in this book have been inspired by everything I have learnt in education over the last 15 years. From trainee teachers and NQTs to middle leaders and my fellow senior leadership teams, you have all inspired me in one way or another. Thank you.

Finally I would like to also thank all of the amazing teachers and educational professionals that I talk to on Twitter. Some of you I have had the pleasure of meeting at conferences and TeachMeets and some I have not. Your incredible desire to make a difference in education far wider than the four walls of your classroom, by sharing ideas and advice, constantly inspires me and has been a big driving force in writing my own book. The opportunity to make a difference inspires us all.

Where possible, I've credited those teachers, authors and other educators who have inspired or created particular ideas featured in this book. You'll find their names dotted throughout, but I'd also like to take the opportunity here to give a special thanks to the following:

Zoë Elder, Director of Education, Clevedon Learning Trust, @fullonlearning;

Paul Dix, Executive Director of Pivotal Education, @pivotalpaul;

Kate Jones, Lead Practitioner Brighton College, @87history;

Simon McLoughlin, @simcloughlin;

Isabella Wallace, Speaker and Author of *Pimp Your Lesson!* and *Talk-Less Teaching;*

John Pacey, Assistant Headteacher;

Jim Smith, Assistant Headteacher, @Jim_Smith;

Mark Anderson, speaker, consultant, author and trainer, @ICTEvangelist;

Jon Bergmann, Flipped Learning Pioneer, @jonbergmann;

Ross Morrison McGill, @TeacherToolkit;

David Mitchell, @DeputyMitchell;

Sarah Ledger, Assistant Headteacher, Teaching and Learning, @sledgerledger;

and

Danielle Bartram, Lead Practitioner, @MissBsResources.

Thank you,

Jon

Introduction

Although the educational landscape and government policy are constantly changing, the ability to engage with young people still remains one of the most important traits that a teacher needs. No matter how intelligent you are, or how much subject-related experience you have, if you can't engage the students in front of you, then you'll have a short shelf life as a teacher. I can still remember the great teachers that taught me at school and some of the not-so-great ones. What stood them apart? The ability to connect with me, to find what lit my fire, floated my boat and made me tick. They were able to motivate me, inspire me and make me laugh and graft in equal measures. They all ultimately found their own way to engage me in their subject.

This is a cookbook-style book with 100 different recipes for engaging the children in your classroom. It is designed so you can pick it up and dip in and out of the ideas whenever you need them, or are looking for a slice of inspiration. Whether it's a class you are struggling with, a dull topic coming up, or you're just looking to spice things up, this book is for you. The ideas are all split into different sections so it's easy for you to navigate your way through the book, either back to front or via a section that takes your fancy.

Although you may have spent your hard-earned money on this book, if you find an idea that works, share it with someone else in your school. The more we can do this as teachers, the better we become. No teacher should feel like they're in it alone – together we are stronger. Also, don't forget that if an idea doesn't work, don't give up on it. There may be a million and one reasons why it didn't work with your Year 9 class on that wet Wednesday afternoon after they came back from PE. Go back to it and try it again with a different class. A quote I heard from behaviour guru Paul Dix recently has stuck with me: 'You are only 30 days away from the school/classroom that you want... it's just that people give up too quickly.'

Whether you're a trainee teacher, an experienced practitioner or somewhere in between, I'd love to hear how you find these ideas and how they may have helped you engage your learners in a different way. Drop me a message, a photo or a blog post of what you are trying via either Twitter @teamtait or on my Facebook education feed – EduTait.

I look forward to connecting with you and hearing your classroom success stories.

How to use this book

This book includes quick, easy, practical ideas for you to dip in and out of, to support you in engaging your students.

Each idea includes:

- a catchy title, easy to refer to and share with your colleagues
- a quote from a teacher or student describing their experiences of the idea that follows or a problem they may have had that using the idea solves
- a summary of the idea in bold, making it easy to flick through the book and identify an idea you want to use at a glance
- a step-by-step guide to implementing the idea.

Each idea also includes one or more of the following:

Teaching tip

Some extra advice on how or how not to run the activity or put the strategy into practice.

Taking it further

Ideas and advice for how to extend the idea or develop it further.

Bonus idea ★

There are 35 bonus ideas in this book that are extra exciting and extra original.

Share how you use these ideas in the classroom and find out what other teachers have done using **#100ideas**.

The classroom

Part 1

Walls for learning

'Make your walls an opportunity for learning, not just an opportunity for wallpaper.'

Think about the walls in your classroom — the same walls that the students either consciously or subconsciously look at every time you teach them. Are they being used as effectively as they could be as a learning resource? Now is the time to put them to good use!

Taking it further

Why not combine this idea with QR code displays (Idea 55) to maximise the impact of your classroom walls? Students could scan these QR codes next to the piece of work to hear you talk about why you have graded it as you have done.

In most classrooms there are the token posters that are loosely connected to that subject, and maybe the odd bit of student work if you are lucky. And if we're completely honest with ourselves, most of the time this is to make the room look nicer rather than having blank magnolia walls all year.

So how can we use these spaces more effectively for learning purposes, rather than just for decoration? It's always good to display aspects of student work on your walls for many different reasons. Firstly, students are usually proud of the fact that their work has made it onto your wall (even if they don't show it). Secondly, it demonstrates your standards to other students and shows that this is what they should be aiming for. However, lots of teachers make the mistake of not capitalising on this further.

Once you have a selection of work on your walls, don't forget to take the opportunity to grade/mark it and then provide reasons for the grade. This way you can then use these as models of excellence for students to aim for, which will keep them much more engaged and motivated.

Fail-safe environment

'We only learn by making mistakes.'

Children usually grow up thinking that making a mistake is bad. We've all seen the tears that come after a mistake has been made, or the reluctance to attempt something challenging because of the fear of getting it wrong. As teachers, it's our job to reverse this process and tell students that it's okay to get things wrong.

We even need to go one step further and tell students that we want them to get things wrong from time to time, because this is the only way that we learn anything. If we go through life getting everything right, then we are not learning – we are just lucky.

Have you ever touched a hot iron? You hurt yourself. Your brain quickly works out what you did wrong and you make sure it doesn't happen again. It's the same in our classrooms. We need to give our students the opportunity to learn from their mistakes in a fail-safe environment.

The best way to promote this 'fail-safe environment' in your classroom is to:

- Always commend students for taking risks.
- Provide overt praise when students try challenging activities and get things wrong.
- Create some posters and wall art promoting the fact that it's okay to make mistakes. Use these images and phrases to subconsciously improve the confidence of your students to tackle challenging tasks.

Teaching tip

Tell your students that it's okay to make mistakes, as long as they don't keep making the same mistakes. Get students to look back through their books every so often at your feedback. Ask them if they can spot any trends. If the same things keep cropping up, then they are not learning.

Room layout

'Variety is the spice of life.'

If your students walk into your classroom and sit in the same seat, as part of the same layout every lesson, it's going to get a bit boring. Why not change it up every so often, so there is a bit of a buzz when they enter the classroom?

Seating plans are very common in classrooms up and down the country now, and teachers are starting to take charge of their classrooms by telling their students where to sit. Most teachers try to change their seating plans throughout the year or after a data capture, to freshen things up. But how often have you changed the entire room layout in your classroom mid-term?

Rows might work for certain activities and group tables might work for others, but there are so many other layout styles that you can use to make a fresh change to your classroom, depending on the size and orientation of your room. Think about whether your activity requires eye contact or student collaboration, and whether the students need to see the board or each other.

In my experience, the moment your students walk into your room and see a completely new layout, they are usually curious and inquisitive about why it's changed, and immediately more engaged than they were when they walked in on countless times before to see the same old layout day after day.

Take more control of your classroom and think about how the layout of your desks can impact on the quality of learning.

Theme your classroom

'Think outside the box. The world is just a canvas for our imagination.'

Building on Idea 3, about changing your room layout from time to time, why not go one step further and theme your room every half term, relating to an area of your syllabus or a topic/unit you are teaching? Be creative and make your classroom a place where students can use their imagination to enhance their learning experience.

No matter what your subject, you can find a way to theme your classroom in relation to a topic or unit you are teaching. Cardboard, old curtains and a pile of boxes can quickly be turned into an ancient Egyptian pyramid or a Sikh temple without much trouble.

However, the very best example of this that I have seen is at Seaham School of Technology in County Durham, where a whole classroom has been devoted to a particular theme. The room is completely taken over and designed with a different theme every half term. Teachers can book 'Room X' for any lesson and can take the students in to see room themes such as 'The Beach', where it's full of sand.

However, for an individual classroom, I would suggest focusing on the front of the room, as this is probably the area that the students focus their attention on the most. Go to your local supermarket for cardboard boxes and maybe your nearest charity shop for old curtains and fabric. Then let your creative juices flow!

Teaching tip

Think about all of the units of work that you will be teaching this year and see which of them naturally lend themselves to a theme that you could create in your classroom. Coming into school for a Saturday morning or for a day in the holidays will give you the time and space to create your masterpiece!

Write on the windows

'Above all else, be daring, be bold, be unconventional.'

The windows in your classroom can also be a hugely valuable learning resource and one that immediately captures the attention of the students! What the students might not know straight away is that your dry wipe pens can be used as effectively on glass as they can be on your board.

It's the unconventional methods that make us sit up in our seats and take notice. Students will automatically be jolted out of their daydreams if they see you doing something that they think you shouldn't. It's this type of activity that absolutely pulls your students in, irrespective of the topic, and engages even the hardest to reach.

All you need is a set of dry wipe markers and you're good to go. It works brilliantly for group work as well. Giving a group a pen and a window to express their thoughts immediately gets them writing (far more quickly than they would have ever committed their thoughts to a piece of A3 sugar paper). The beauty of this method is that it also immediately creates a gallery of everyone's work high enough for everybody to see and read it. No need to try and pin up everyone's sheets or get them to hold them up as they are speaking. This is all taken care of by the fact that your windows are visible to everyone.

Before you (or your cleaner) wipe away all of the great work your students have done on the windows, make sure you take some photos of the work, which you can use for a variety of reasons, especially for evidence of progress.

Make a whiteboard anywhere

'You can't use up creativity, the more the use, the more you have!'

Whiteboard paint is a great way of creating multiple whiteboards for either individual creativity or group collaboration.

We all know that most students hate getting things wrong in their books. This creates an environment where some students are then reluctant to spell difficult words or answer challenging questions in the fear that it will make their work look untidy. But if these students had somewhere to practise their spellings, or draft a quick answer, would it give them more confidence?

With whiteboard paint, you can paint over any flat surface to create a whiteboard that can be used with normal dry wipe pens. You can paint an A4-size corner of each student desk so that they always have a space to draft, jot notes down or practise their spelling of keywords, ready to rub off whenever they choose.

Whiteboard paint can be used in all sorts of creative and beneficial ways, such as:

- Remove old noticeboards in classrooms and paint the area with whiteboard paint to enable it to become a collaborative group-work/mind-mapping board.
- Paint the back of classroom doors so that it becomes a creative learning space.
- Paint an area of your classroom wall and stick QR codes on (see Idea 55), which link to short video clips about your topic. Students can then write their thoughts around the QR code.
- Paint an area of the floor in an art room so that it becomes a giant canvas promoting mass collaboration.

Taking it further

Students may also want to use the new whiteboards on their desks to write down their own personal targets for that lesson, so they're always in their eye line. This way they feel they have a real ownership of the target, as it's right there in front of them on their desk and can be changed at any point.

The bigger picture

Part 2

Make it relevant

'We have to keep transforming ourselves to stay relevant for the future.'

Far too often students ask, 'What's the point of this?' because they fail to see the relevance of what they are doing. You need to make your subject content relevant to your students so that they can engage with it.

Relevance to young people is key if you want them to really buy into what you are doing. They need to feel that it 'has a point' and that it's going to benefit them. Many teachers in many subjects have had to cover content that is seemingly meaningless to the young people of today. However, the shift towards a more skills-based curriculum has given teachers more licence than ever to use content and scenarios that are relevant to today's children, so that they can engage them in their learning far more easily.

My top tips for making your subject content more relevant are:

- Find out the interests of your students.
- Use these topics or interests to build your lesson around.
- Get your students to demonstrate the skills that you have been teaching them, using the topics they are interested in.

If you ask a disengaged student to write a two-page essay on Macbeth to demonstrate their knowledge and effective use of subordinate clauses, you'll probably get some resistance. By simply changing the emphasis and asking them to write a two-page match review of their favourite football team, ensuring they demonstrate the correct use of subordinate clauses, you'll probably find a much warmer response.

Make it real

'Make it real, make it something they can touch or feel in their heart.'

Authentic learning experiences are crucial if we want students to really feel their learning. These are the moments where students make deep learning connections and that they will remember long after leaving your classroom.

We can all get students to learn from a book or via a YouTube clip, or even retell a story that has been passed on between many mouths. But get someone to talk to your students about a personal experience, or someone (even you) who can share emotions that are linked to a story, and you start to create a magical learning environment that students can really relate to.

Students remember real people, they remember real stories and they certainly always remember real emotions. Whenever you can, try to tap into real people who can give authentic accounts of parts of your syllabus. You could talk about hurricanes in geography, but imagine the extra engagement if you could get somebody to tell the real story of when they had to leave their home and run for safety in the eye of a storm...

You can also make subject content real by linking your lessons to things that are happening in the real world. This will not only engage your students in their learning, but will also provide you with many opportunities to use the countless quotes, photos, videos and articles that are freely available on the Internet.

Teaching tip

Keep an eye on the news and look for opportunities on websites such as Reuters to use powerful images of global news stories that might make your students take note and sit up and listen. There shouldn't be a week that passes without you being able to link your subject to some big news story.

Taking it further

If you are going to get students to write a letter to somebody, make sure you actually send it! Don't just do it as a paper exercise, which you might use to put up on your wall; get the students to write it and send it. If they know it will actually be read by that person, they are far more likely to make sure it's a well-written letter.

Make it local

'We understand more of the things we are closer to, because we can feel their impact on our lives.'

There are so many ways in which you can make your subject become even more real to your students by linking it to something local. If your students understand the context and it is part of their local or family heritage, then there is far more chance of significant engagement not just by the student, but by the whole family.

Every town or village has history, culture and newsworthy events that happen all of the time. If you can use this to provide the subject content or context in your lessons, then you'll be on to a winner with the whole community.

The best example of this I have ever seen was an example that Ron Berger wrote about in his book *An Ethic of Excellence*. Ron talks about how his students had to do a project on water clarity and it fit in perfectly with an issue that the town was having with radon testing. The students carried out experiments on the town's water and even wrote a comprehensive report for the town council about what the town needed to do in order to make the water safe for consumption by the local residents.

The beauty of this project was that all of the students lived in the town, so their report was actually going to benefit the lives and well-being of their own families. The motivation to do well went through the roof! Imagine if your own students got involved in a project about their own town or school. Your local council website should have information about what's going on.

Bonus idea ★

Why not contact your local town council to see what projects your students might be able to get involved in and maybe even contribute towards? You might even be able to bring in some expert help to assist with your delivery of the project in your classroom.

De-bloomify your objectives

'Sometimes you have to look at the bigger picture to understand the finer details.' Credit to Zoë Elder, Director of Education, Clevedon Learning Trust, @fullonlearning for this idea.

Lesson objectives are now a common fixture in classrooms up and down the country, but how often do your students know why you are doing what you are doing? Take the time to simplify and talk through your objectives so that students see the bigger picture of their learning.

The crime that lots of teachers commit is to write their lesson objectives for an audience of Ofsted or a senior leader during an observation. Seldom are they written in language that a bottom set of 11-year-olds can understand, and that can enable them to tell you midway through the lesson what they are doing and why.

My advice would be to remove the need to include 'Bloom's taxonomy'. Don't get me wrong – it's great to think about how or whether you are going to stretch your students by using higher order thinking skills. But telling your students that they are going to have to 'synthesise' something is a complete waste of time.

Instead, I would take the approach of using what Zoe Elder calls the 'so that' of learning. Write out your objective in simple terms that the students will understand, followed by the statement 'so that...', which then needs to be followed by why you are doing what you are doing today. Put simply, if you can't work out what to write after the two words 'so that', then you need to really think about why you are doing it in the first place!

> **Taking it further**
>
> Instead of merely placing your objectives on the whiteboard at the beginning of your lesson, get your students to read through them and make personal sense of them. Midway through your lesson, randomly ask your students what they are doing today and why. If they can't answer you, your objectives have had little or no impact on their learning.

Student-created success criteria

'Take ownership of your success.'

Success criteria have been a welcome addition to most classrooms, enabling students to see what they need to do in order to be successful. But rather than spoon-feeding your students this information, why not get them to come up with their own criteria once they understand the task brief?

Teaching tip

You could rotate the students or groups of students who design the success criteria for the rest of the class each lesson. This way a group of students can report to the class about what they all have to do to be successful, thus creating a collaborative approach to the ownership of their learning.

We constantly tell students what to do and what they have to do in order to pass a task, a test or an examination. But if we want our students to take real ownership of their learning, we need to give them more opportunities to work this out for themselves, rather than just doing things because they have been told to do them.

A great way of doing this is to provide the students with a question or task, along with the relevant section of the exam board specification, broken down into student-friendly language. The students can then work out for themselves, or as part of a group, exactly what the exam board is looking for and the skills or content that they need to evidence or provide in order to be successful.

This way you will avoid comments like 'Why do we have to do this?' or 'I'm not bothered about doing that', because your students will start doing things for themselves in a more intrinsic way and not just because you have told them to do so.

Structure

Part 3

Meet and greet

'Building connections, developing relationships.' Credit to Paul Dix, @pivotalpaul for this idea.

Never underestimate the power of a handshake and the power of physical human connection. Getting the opportunity to shake every student's hand in your class as they enter the room sends out a strong message that everyone is respected and everyone matters.

A simple handshake can convey so much without you even having to open your mouth. Firstly, it is a physical sign of a mutual agreement between student and teacher – a sign that, without having to say a word, shows that the teacher is respecting the student. In return, it is a signal that the student is respecting the teacher's expectations and classroom rules. Secondly, it demonstrates that everyone matters. There are no favourites or groups of students who seem to get along with the teacher better than anyone else. Everyone is greeted and everyone is valued as much as the next person.

Standing at the door as your students arrive lets you meet and greet everyone with a handshake, without any fuss or extra work. This also enables you to look them in the eye and greet them with a couple of nice words. Using their name makes it very personal, shows you know them and tells them you care about them. For some students, you might even be able to stretch this to a couple of sentences about which subject they've just come from or even what they've been up to at the weekend. Whatever you say, it conveys the simple messages of 'I care about you', 'I know you' and 'You know what I expect from you during the next hour'.

Photo starters

'A picture paints a thousand words.'

Powerful photographs can shock, inspire and make students sit up and think in equal measures. Every picture can also mean so many different things to so many different people. They are perfect to spark discussion and to help you engage your students in a new topic or unit.

We've all heard the phrase 'a picture paints a thousand words' and it's true. Photographs can tell you so many things just from one still image. Students can ask questions, make comments and try to work out what is happening and why it might be linked to their lesson today. If you are looking for something to promote curious and inquisitive learners, then this is it.

Due to the advances in modern technology, high-quality, powerful images are freely available every minute of every day via most press agencies, direct from their photographers across the world. The best places to search are websites such as Reuters, which gather the very best photographs from world events as they happen. You can be sure to find what you need here if it's happened recently in the world.

The best way to use 'photo starters' is:

1 Put the photo up on your whiteboard, full screen, as the students enter the room.
2 Give the students time to look at it and ponder its relevance while you take the register.
3 Ask students what is happening in the photo and whether they have any questions about it.
4 Ask students to work out the relevance of the photo in connection with their learning.

Teaching tip

Ensure your students think deeply about the image on your board. Allow a moment of silence for students to focus on the image without distractions. Students may find lots of different stories and connections in the photos, so be prepared to explore these thoughts with them.

Here's the answer, what's the question?

'Can you guess what I'm thinking?'

As teachers, we ask up to 400 questions per day, but how many times do you tell students the answer and get them to work out the question? Try flipping your questioning on its head, like they do on *Have I Got News For You*, and start to have a bit more fun with your questions.

A great way to start your lesson is to put up a number or a random answer on the board and get students to think about what the question may be. You can make it more or less challenging by either telling the students the topic it relates to or just throwing it out there without any guidance whatsoever. Imagine walking into a classroom and seeing a number like 256 on the board and being asked what the question is!

This can create a lot of fun in your lessons, so be prepared to accept funny and unusual answers from your students without getting uptight about it. If you've watched *Have I Got News For You* before, you'll already know the random and hilarious answers that are given for a few minutes before the actual answer is arrived upon! Students will come to really enjoy this segment of your lesson and begin to engage in the fun. You might even find your students interpret the answer in lots of educational ways that you never expected!

Fill in the blanks

'Too often we don't give people the opportunity to fill in the blanks.'

Lesson objectives can just become part of the wallpaper in many classrooms, with students hardly taking any notice of them. If you want your students to really understand objectives and their importance, you need to get them to do something with them.

Just getting students to read through your objectives every lesson or even write them down in their books is simply not enough. Ask most students midway through your lesson what the objective of the lesson is (without letting them refer back to it in their books) and you might get a bit of a shock. In my experience, most students struggle to tell you what you spent the key part of your lesson talking about!

Try removing certain keywords from your lesson objectives and then get your students to read them and work out what is missing. This way, they will have to completely understand not only the objective, but also how it fits in with the bigger picture of their learning journey. The more challenging you want to make the activity, depending on the year or ability group, the more words you can remove at any given time. If you build this in as part of your daily routine, you'll soon get your students taking a far more active part in their learning and using the lesson objective as a way to really think about what they are doing, rather than it just going in one ear and out the other.

Taking it further

Write your lesson objective out in very basic language, without including any subject-specific keywords. Once your students understand what they are doing in the lesson, ask them to improve the objective by adding key language and improving the content overall.

Emoji objectives

'Crack the code to work out what we are doing today.' Credit to Kate Jones, Lead Practitioner Brighton College, @87history for this idea.

Emojis are now fast becoming a cultural part of the way we communicate. Our students understand them, so why not spice up your objectives from time to time by writing them as part of an emoji code that they need to crack?

Taking it further

You can download whole sets of emoji icons from various places on the Internet. A quick search in Google will get you started. Once you've got a set downloaded, start separating them into distinctive folders based on their categories, for ease of use when you design your next objective.

As previously stated, the lesson objectives that you share with your students can become just like wallpaper unless you are prepared to do something different with them. Why not try changing your lesson objectives to include the use of emojis? Students then have to read the objective and break down the emoji code so that they can establish what they are learning that day.

My top tips for creating emoji lesson objectives are:

1 Find a lesson objective that you are about to use in one of your lessons.
2 Think about the emojis that could be used to describe the activities that you have planned.
3 Replace as many words as you can with emoji icons.
4 Include this new emoji code on your PowerPoint or lesson presentation.

Don't worry if other adults can't crack the code. In my experience in using these emoji-styled objectives, none of the adults that I showed could work it out! It made me worried that none of the students would be able to understand what we were doing. However, when showing my classes, the students usually got it in ten seconds or less!

Emoji exit tickets

'Your comments are extremely useful to us.' Credit to Kate Jones, Lead Practitioner Brighton College, @87history for this idea.

How often do you ask the students what they thought of your lesson or what they think they have learned in the last 60 minutes with you? By getting them to fill out an exit ticket before they leave, you can gain a valuable insight into how successful your lesson has been.

The idea of using exit tickets as a method of finding out how students have found your lesson has been around for a while now, and it's a superb way to get student feedback. However, in my experience, students often just write down a few buzz words on the exit ticket and think of it as more of a test that they have to get the right answer to.

By using emojis, you can ask the students how they have found the last unit of work or the last lesson. Students are asked to circle the emoji or emojis that best reflect how they have felt, thus finding out whether they felt happy, sad, challenged, stressed, tearful, etc.

When creating your emoji exit ticket, ensure that you have a good mix of emojis, which captures as many emotions as possible, so that your students can express themselves truthfully rather than just telling you what you want to hear. You can download full sets of emojis with a simple search in Google.

Taking it further

Get students to stick their exit tickets in their book after each unit of work so that you can quickly review how they found each topic across the year when flicking through their book.

Bonus idea

Why not create entry tickets that are the same as your exit tickets, but that are used to see how each student feels about a new topic, or after a pre-assessment activity. This way you can compare both the entry and exit ticket after the unit and see the difference in how they now feel about the topic.

Tweet your learning

'If you can't explain it simply, then you don't know it well enough.'

Another great strategy to get students to summarise their learning is to ask them to 'Tweet' what they have just learned in your lesson in under a certain amount of words, thus forcing them to be succinct and accurate with their summary.

Taking it further

As a form of differentiation in a mixed ability group, why not give different word limits to different groups of learners? You may find that giving a group of students a higher limit makes it either easier to achieve, or harder!

One of the biggest problems when students sit examinations is that they sometimes see an exam question worth three or four marks and then just ramble on for three or four sentences without getting to the point. Making our students strip everything back to the nitty gritty is a key skill, which we sometimes forget.

Most students will know that on Twitter you can only type a Tweet with a maximum of 140 characters, thus forcing you to be succinct. Try this with your students when you ask them to summarise their learning. Ask them to use a maximum of 140 characters, or maybe just give them a maximum word count of 25 words.

The best examples I have seen of this are where mobile phone templates have been printed out and students have to 'Tweet their Learning' on the screen of the mobile phone in the word limit dictated by the teacher. The phone template can then be stuck in their books as a record of the learning that happened in that lesson.

A quick search in Google using the words 'mobile phone template' will give you templates that you can save and print.

Plenary professors

'Knowledge is of no value unless you put it into practice.'

As trainee teachers, we've all been taught at some stage or another to summarise the key points of the lesson and the learning that has taken place. However, this is all done from your perspective, not the students'. Get one of your students to deliver the plenary for the class.

'Plenary professors' are great for getting students to take a big part in the teaching and learning process, and also for you to see what your lesson has actually delivered from the students' point of view and not just what it says in your lesson plan.

The best use of this idea that I have seen came from an English teacher who had a rota that determined who the plenary professor was going to be each lesson. At the beginning, the class were informed of who the plenary professor was going to be and then, in the last five minutes of the lesson, that student delivered the plenary to the whole class.

Benefits of using plenary professors:

- Students who are selected feel far more part of the lesson.
- The student who is selected each lesson must really engage with the lesson and the content if they are to deliver a plenary to the whole class on what the lesson was about.
- It gives students the confidence to express what they have learned, whilst also helping others to summarise the key points of the lesson.

Taking it further

Why not go the extra mile and get hold of a mortar board that the student has to wear whilst they are delivering the plenary, or even let them wear it through the whole lesson if they want to? Most students love this kind of thing and it's a way to make learning fun and engaging.

Just a minute

'Your time starts now.'

Getting students to summarise their learning is an important part of their reflective learning journey. Being able to articulate what they have done and why they have done it to you and their fellow peers in only one minute is not only challenging, but competitive too.

Ask your students to talk for a whole minute without stopping, pausing or repeating themselves. This develops their ability to be succinct, but with enough detail and explanation to keep everyone else engaged.

To do this, students need to be more self-aware of their own learning journey and more engaged in the lesson content, so that they can talk freely about the finer details of the lesson.

Don't be surprised, though, when you first try this, if your students really struggle. They might require a framework to help them structure their minute. A basic structure like the one below will not only help them complete their one minute challenge, but will also help everyone understand what they are doing and why:

1 Name three things you have done today.
2 Why have you been doing what you are doing?
3 How does today's lesson link into the bigger picture?
4 What new learning have you now got that you didn't have when you entered the classroom earlier?

Select a random student to take the challenge at the end of each lesson, so that the whole class knows they need to be thinking about the questions throughout the lesson.

Delivery

Part 4

Be real

'Open the door and let them in a little.'

Most of the time, students don't see us as real people. They don't think we have lives outside of school and probably assume that we have a sleeping bag in our classrooms and never leave the building. By giving a little away about who you are and what you do outside of school, you'll be sure to get a lot back in terms of trust and respect from your students.

Bonus idea ★

Once you've offered a little about you, make sure to find out something about your students, especially the ones that you know you'll need to work hard at building a positive relationship with. Once you've done this, use it as a conversation starter around the school site when you see them to help break down barriers.

I once heard a saying that has always rung true for me: 'students don't learn from people they don't like'. This does not mean you have to be everyone's best friend – far from it. However, when you stop to think about the teachers that you learned most from at school, it was probably the ones who you got to know really well and the ones you could have a bit of a conversation with – the ones who, if you bumped into them in the street now, you'd be happy to stop and say 'hi' to.

Being real to your students means telling them a little about you. A few small details that you feel comfortable with is all they need to get to know you. You might tell them that you have children of your own or which football team you support or even the music you like to listen to. These tiny bits of information don't do anything to compromise your authority or professional standing in the class, but it helps students to start to see you as a real person.

It also gives you valuable topics of conversation to tap into if you are trying to engage some of your harder-to-reach students. For example, being able to chat to some of your more difficult boys about the football at the weekend might just be the way in that you need to start buying some much-needed currency with them.

Command spot

'If you command wisely, you'll be obeyed cheerfully.'

As teachers, we are constantly wandering around the classroom and, because of this, we sometimes find it hard to gain the attention of our students quickly. Pick a command spot in your classroom where, whenever you stand on that spot, your students know you are about to address them.

Although this sounds like a fairly simple thing to do, it can have a major impact on your delivery and your ease of being able to grab the attention of your class when you want to address them and deliver a key teaching point or a set of instructions. It's like the way you may have seen a teacher put their hand in the air and wait for all the students to be quiet before they begin to speak.

If you train your students to notice when you are standing on your command spot, you'll significantly decrease the number of times you have to battle with your class to be quiet so that you can provide some expert input for them – a potential lifesaver for your voice in the run up to Christmas in that long, hard first term!

Tips on making it work:

1 Pick a spot in your classroom that you wouldn't usually stand in to do mundane tasks like taking the register, etc.
2 Stand on that spot and tell your students that whenever you stand there, you are about to address them.
3 Tell your students that when they spot you standing there, they should stop what they are doing and listen.
4 Test it out randomly throughout the next few lessons to embed it into your own and your students' daily classroom routines.

Teaching tip

Try to pick a spot in your classroom that is a little bit different from where you would normally stand, but one where the students can still see you without having to turn around or move their chairs. The less movement or fuss required, the better.

Bonus idea ★

If you feel your command spot becomes a bit repetitive over time, why not change it every term or half term to keep it fresh? You might want to change it every time you change your seating plan, so that you're always keeping your students on their toes.

Pitch, tone and volume

'The volume of your voice does not increase the validity of your argument.'

Battling to make yourself heard with a group of disengaged 13-year-olds can be very difficult, especially for the less experienced, but sometimes raising your voice isn't the answer. Try varying your pitch, tone and volume every so often to re-engage your class.

To the uneducated eye, being loud means you're in control. However, the more experienced amongst us will tell you that a loud teacher produces a loud class. Just like we copy body language, students will naturally adapt to their environment, and the louder you are, the louder they will become. Try lowering your volume for long periods of your lesson and speaking much more softly to your students – watch them naturally lower their own volume.

Varying your pitch and tone can also have a dramatic effect on your delivery. If your default delivery is monotone then your students will soon lose interest, as they will believe you have no real enthusiasm for the lesson and lack a distinct passion for your subject.

Try to work far more expression into your voice, like a newsreader, narrator or chat show host. Start to emphasise key words with added volume and use your voice to add more meaning, excitement and curiosity to your questioning.

Once you have cracked how to vary your voice, use it to suddenly change the emphasis of a lesson or jolt your students out of their seats every now and again. Your voice might just be the engaging tool that you've been looking for!

The dramatic pause

'Never forget the power of silence.'

It's not always about the sound of our own voice. Periods of silence can be extremely powerful, especially when carefully and strategically placed at the right time. You can get your students on the edge of their seats, just by adding a dramatic pause every now and again.

We've seen it so many times before: the killer line in a movie, which is spoken with such dramatic effect. A brief pause between lines, which can feel like an eternity and creates such tension and curiosity that it grips us. Using this technique in our classrooms can be the perfect tool when we want to create that healthy tension, thus really making our students hang on our every word, waiting for that key piece of information or answer.

This technique probably doesn't come naturally, so it will rely on you practising it. Think of yourself as a film star, practising your lines in front of a mirror. The more you do this, the more comfortable you will be with those previously awkward seconds of silence.

By pausing at the most important parts of your delivery, or set of key instructions, you are naturally adding a point of emphasis. Students will begin to take far more notice of what you have just said, learning to create mental bookmarks in their head, rather than those key points getting lost within a long set of instructions.

Taking it further

Learn to use your pause points as complete periods of silence, without filling them with your natural silence fillers such as 'umm' and 'err'. Instead, recognise these words as your default fillers and consciously work on not saying them when you plan to pause.

Bonus idea ★

Take a look at some of the best movie scenes ever filmed and watch how the actors deliver their key lines. Watch for dramatic pause points and start to think about how you can incorporate these into your lessons.

Excitement is contagious

'Learning is not a spectator sport, so let's play!'

Learning can be tough at times and some of the content we have to deliver can be fairly dull. But that doesn't mean that we can't inject an element of fun and excitement into our lessons from time to time.

Teaching tip

Even if your plan is the most exciting plan that the world has ever seen, you will not convince your students to 'buy in' to the excitement if you are not feeling it yourself. Let go of yourself and dive in with bucketloads of enthusiasm and you'll be certain to get the same in return from your students.

Think back to whenever you have spoken to anyone boring. It doesn't matter if they are telling you that you've just won a free trip to Disneyland – you'd probably fail to believe them. On the other hand, speak to someone super-excited and enthusiastic who's telling you that you could win that trip, and you'll probably be getting all excited and ready to pack your case!

Your students will naturally pick up on how keen you are on certain topics or units that you teach, so it's important not to show your true colours if there is a topic you are less than enthusiastic about teaching. Don't be surprised or annoyed at your students if they are lethargic or less than forthcoming with energy if you are not at the top of your game. Remember that an enthusiastic teacher equals enthusiastic students!

Top tips for making your lessons exciting:

- Build the students up into a frenzy about the exciting nature of today's lesson.
- Talk like you have been waiting for this lesson to come around for weeks!
- Change the room layout.
- Bring in a strange or random artefact as part of the lesson.
- Tell your students that you're breaking away from the scripted lesson to do something amazing and exciting (even if it's part of the script).

Get dressed up!

'Show me, don't just tell me.'

When actors play characters on stage, they get dressed up to be more authentic to their audience. Have you ever imagined what it could do to your lessons if you turned up dressed as one of the characters from a period or novel that you were teaching your students?

Students love a bit of fun thrown into their lessons and they love the unexpected. As they arrive for school that day, they will have absolutely no idea that your lesson will be any different from the norm. But what if they see you earlier in the day, on break duty or in the corridor, dressed up in costume? What if they realise that the costume you are wearing is related to a character or famous person that you have been learning about? Imagine their intrigue and excitement leading up to your lesson!

Getting dressed up can give your lesson not only a huge slice of fun, but also some much-needed authenticity. Talking about a character or time period when you are dressed up accordingly can really help spark your students' imaginations. They can not only hear what you are telling them, but they can also now see it. Connecting these two learning paths together can make for far deeper learning, and you can be sure that your students will remember this lesson!

Teaching tip

As with a lot of other tips in this book, this is a strategy to be used sparingly. It will not only lose its appeal if you are dressed up in a different costume every other lesson, but your colleagues might also think you are going slightly mad!

Taking it further

Why not get a colleague to take the first five minutes of your lesson, introducing the topic or character – then you can suddenly enter the classroom in your costume at the perfect moment! Imagine the drama as you burst in right on cue!

Help! I'm being held hostage!

'I'm a teacher, get me out of here!' Credit to Simon McLoughlin, @simcloughlin for this idea.

Cover lessons can sometimes be really boring for students when you're not there but, with a little bit of pre-planning and creative thought, you can spice up the delivery for the cover teacher with a pre-recorded video in a strange location!

Teaching tip

Although you will want to make the video clip engaging and realistic, don't go overboard and make it too authentic. The last thing you want is students going home and phoning the police because they have been traumatised by your apparent kidnapping!

Taking it further

If it's something your students loved when you did it the first time, make sure it's something you do every time you are not there to teach them. Change the location and story behind why you are not with them today.

For most teachers, cover work is planned and left the night before via an email or a set of instructions taped to the desk... but I imagine that, if you are reading this book for inspiration, you don't want to be just any other teacher! With a bit of thought and creativity, you can record a video for your students that can be played at the start of the lesson by any cover teacher.

The idea is to pretend to be taken hostage somewhere, and that you have been given the opportunity to record a video message for a loved one. However, you have chosen to use your message to tell your students what work they have to do whilst you are trying to escape! Tell your students that, because you are so committed to their education, you felt that this was the best use of your one message!

For best results and drama, try to film your video in a strange location, not just sat at your desk in school. Make it a little bit more realistic, maybe with some dim lighting and possibly not looking your usual best. The video only needs to be brief, explaining what the students need to do in the lesson, and can be easily filmed via your phone, tablet or webcam.

Models of excellence

'Try before you buy.'

We all like to see what we're buying before we buy it and I'm sure we all look at the picture on the front of the box before we build a bit of flat-pack furniture. Our students need to see this as well. Just like us, they need to see what it's going to look like, sound like or feel like before they invest their time and effort in something.

Although we try to be as clear as we can in our instructions, we will always find some students or some classes that just don't have the same vision for what the finished task will look like as we do. Using models of excellence gives you a great opportunity to be very explicit about the standards that you expect and the finer details that need to be included.

Not only does this engage students, because they can see exactly what you are looking for, but it also gives them the opportunity – now they've seen what an example looks like – to go above and beyond your initial expectations. What better way to impress your teacher and show off your knowledge of a subject than to go one step further than the example that the teacher held up as a model of excellence.

It's never been easier to gather, store and retrieve models of excellence these days. A few years ago, you'd have to keep files and files of paper and shelves of artefacts, and dust them down when you brought them out of your cupboard. With the advances in technology and digital files, and with photographs so easy to take, create and store, you can keep as many different models of excellence as you wish.

Teaching tip

Be careful not to show a class a model of excellence that is too close to what they are about to do. You might just find that all of their work is mysteriously similar to the model that you gave them.

Taking it further

As a motivation strategy, tell students that the best three pieces of work will become the models of excellence that you will show your classes next year.

I've got you covered

'We've got everything you need.'

If you want students to be successful and completely engaged in an activity, make sure you can give them the very best equipment and resources to do the job. Some students might not have the best stationery in their pencil case, so this might just be the incentive they need.

Imagine the student in your art lesson who needs to be precise in their sketches, but the only pencil they have in their blazer pocket is a blunt one they found on the corridor floor this morning. Their experience of drawing has always been limited, due to the lack of quality equipment at their disposal. Watch their engagement rise when they are given the right tools to do the job. Watch how they start to see the difference that a good, sharp drawing pencil can make to a piece of artwork.

Similarly, when getting students to take notes so they can pick out key vocabulary at a later date, why not provide pots of highlighters on desks so that students can use these whenever they want to highlight key words and keep their books looking smart?

By providing the necessary and high-quality equipment for students, you are doing two things:

1 Firstly, you are showing your students that in your class, you will go the extra mile for them and, in return, you expect hard work.
2 Secondly, you are giving every child in your class the opportunity to be successful, irrespective of their personal circumstances.

Poundland pedagogy

'Cheap as chips!' Credit to Isabella Wallace, Author and Speaker, for this idea.

Not all great classroom ideas and resources have to cost you a packet. In fact, some of the most creative and imaginative resources can be picked up from stores such as Poundland for next to nothing. Get your creative hat on and go shopping!

We sometimes fall into the trap of thinking that we have to spend hundreds or sometimes thousands of pounds to engage our students with new shiny technology. But if we stop to look around us at the creative ways in which we can use some of the most basic and random of objects, we might just find that we can spice up our lesson delivery on a shoestring budget.

Not only will the items serve to put a different spin on your lessons, but the students are also bound to be intrigued and curious about what you've bought and how it is going to be used in today's lesson.

Making learning fun is not about dumbing it down, but instead making it something that the students want to engage in and something they'll remember for more than five minutes after they leave our classrooms. With this kind of approach, even the most disengaged and hard-to-reach students can't help but be engaged in the exciting learning that is taking place.

Next time you're out shopping, pop into a bargain store and think about all the different ways that you can use some of the items on the shelves to engage the students in your class. See what you can get for £5 that might be the answer you've been looking for to make a fairly dull topic come to life.

Taking it further

Why not set a challenge with members of your department, where you all have to incorporate an item (or series of items) that you buy for each other into your lessons this week? Each person can be set a £5 limit. You just never know what learning opportunities will be created!

Keep it bite-sized

'When problems seem too big, break them up into smaller chunks.'

Students can often disengage with tasks that go on for too long. For best results and optimum engagement, chunk your tasks into shorter, bite-sized time slots with regular checkpoints.

Set most students off on a 15-minute task and they'll feel completely in their comfort zone. Time will gradually drift away and, before they know it, they will have used up a third of their time without the evidence to prove that the time has been worth it. By breaking a 15-minute task down into three five-minute, bite-sized chunks, this lets you create a checkpoint to see where everyone is at. Your checkpoint may also have a set of points that the students must have covered in this time. If these checkpoints are shared with the students before they start, it's far easier for them to stay on track and up to speed.

Longer tasks are also one of the reasons why so many students disengage in lessons. Breaking these tasks down tackles two key issues:

1 A student has so much work to do in the activity that they don't know where to start or what to do first. They spend too much time worrying about how much they have to do because it all seems too much for them. In this instance, breaking it down into manageable chunks of time and tasks helps them focus and stay on track.

2 A student realises that they are going to finish their task way in advance of the set time limit, so begins to disengage because the challenge level is not there for them. In this instance, regular checkpoints would have highlighted this to the teacher early on, so they can be set an extension task to hold their engagement.

Speed dating

'Trust me, I'm a teacher.'

We all know that when you have to teach something to someone else, you need to know it inside out. Suddenly, there is a greater motivation to learn it, because you don't want to let someone else down, or be caught out demonstrating that you don't know your stuff!

The speed dating method is great to allow students to turn into student teachers and become experts in a certain part of the curriculum. By giving your students the opportunity to become experts in certain areas and teach their peers, they can become far more engaged in their learning. It also gives students far more responsibility for their learning, because they are now not just learning it for their own benefit, but for someone else's.

This activity works especially well to engage students in their revision. Each student is given a different topic to study and become an expert in. Students then move around the room in short intervals, sharing or learning a different topic with each 'date'.

1 Once the buzzer sounds, students then listen to their date teach them for another allotted period of time before moving on to another 'date'.
2 Each student has a set amount of time to teach their 'date' about their area of expertise.
3 Set a visual timer on the whiteboard so everyone can see the allotted time ticking down.

To increase the pace and challenge of speed dating for different year groups or ability groups, the time allocated to each date can be shortened or lengthened.

> **Teaching tip**
>
> Have a prescribed rotation formula for how your dates move around the room. This will stop students from just going to sit with their friends and others saying they've already spoken to the only people that are left without a date.

Questioning

Part 5

Wait time

'I've got a question, so I want an answer... quick!'

The average wait time that teachers give before accepting an answer is one second! We need to give students more time to think before answering our questions.

When you stop and think about it, we've all done it. We ask a question, a student immediately puts their hand up and we accept the first thing that comes out of their mouth. But how can this be a carefully thought-out answer if we are prepared to accept an answer in approximately one second? Would you be happy to give your very best answer if you were told that you had to respond to a particularly challenging task with no thinking time?

If you want well-thought-out answers, start training your class in wait time. Make sure your class know that you will be giving three, four or five seconds before accepting any answers. This will not only improve the length, quality and depth of the answers that you receive, but it will also enable more students to think and participate in your questioning, rather than it being like a 'faster finger first' quiz game, which most students get fed up with rather quickly if you keep going to the same students for the answers.

If you build in regular wait time in your questioning as part of your daily routines, your students will soon learn to think deeply whenever you ask a question, and the responses you receive will be of far higher quality.

Hands-down hot seating

'I'm coming to you next.'

If you only accept answers from the students who have their hands up, you are letting certain students opt out of your questioning. You'll find in most classes that it's the same students who put their hands up and the same ones who'd rather not. Take control of who answers the questions in your class by not allowing any hands up.

Search the Internet for any picture of a teacher in a classroom and you'll probably find an image of children with their hands up in class. It is synonymous with what most people think about questioning. But if you are only going to take answers from the students who have their hands up as your default setting, then pretty quickly the students who don't want to think or participate work out what to do for an easy ride.

Try flipping this on its head and tell your students that there is now a 'no hands up' rule. Once you have asked a question and given sufficient wait time (see Idea 33), you will now select who will answer that question. This is great for four reasons:

1 Everyone in your class has to think of the answer to the question, not just the ones who wanted to put their hands up... nobody knows who's going to be asked to answer it!

2 You can ensure that all of your students are participating in your questioning.

3 You can target your pupil premium or SEN students if required.

4 You can start off by asking a lower ability student to begin to answer the question, before asking someone of a higher ability to add or build on it (see Idea 36).

Taking it further

Try combining this method with Wait time (Idea 33), The ABC of Questioning (Idea 36) and even Random name generator (Idea 35) to truly make you the king of questioning in your classroom!

Bonus idea ★

When planning your lesson, highlight specific students on your seating plan whom you are going to target that lesson for questioning. This way you can be very strategic in your questioning, using it as a dynamic assessment for learning tool to gauge understanding and progress.

Random name generator

'The suspense is killing me!'

Once you've taken to a 'Hands-down hot seating' approach (Idea 34), why not spice it up a little by using a random name generator to randomly select who is going to answer the next question?

From time to time, we all love a bit of suspense – and our students are no different. The ability to randomly select who is going to answer the next question you ask builds healthy tension in your classroom and can make your questioning come to life!

Random name generators can be found all over the Internet and require little preparation for even the busiest of classroom teachers. All you need to do is to input the names of your students into the name generator and then you are free to use it right away.

For the best impact, search for a name generator that you can download and save multiple copies of. This way, you can have one for each class you teach, meaning you only have to pre-load the students' names once at the start of the year. Be creative in your search for different name generators as well. Remember that even your most amazing ideas will become the norm after a while. There are lots of different styles of name generators out there, so try changing to a different design after a while. Just search for 'name selector' in Google and you'll come across a wide selection.

The ABC of questioning

'A, B, C – it's easy as 1, 2, 3!'

Can you get your students to collaborate on answers by Adding to or Building on an answer? Or maybe they can even Challenge it?

We sometimes fall into the trap of accepting the first answer that comes our way in our classrooms. But it takes a little bit more experience and composure to hold out for a better answer before we step in and reframe the first student's answer in our own words.

Try to resist the urge to do this and, instead of accepting the first answer, ask the class if someone would like to **Add** to the answer or **Build** on it. This way you are promoting collaborative learning in the following ways:

- Students start to listen to everyone else's answers to see whether they can add value to it.
- An initial response to a question gets added to and built on, so that it becomes a well-thought-out and highly constructed answer that hits all of the success criteria for a top grade.
- Students who give a lower ability answer, or are not sure of the answer, get to hear other people add to it, enabling them to learn from their peers about how to construct a great answer.

Every now and again, throw in a curve ball. Even if an answer you have been given is correct, ask the class if they would like to **Challenge** it. Being asked to challenge an answer that you thought was correct really makes you stop and think.

Teaching tip

Set the ground rules at the start of the year so that students respect each other's answers, and to ensure that, if they are Adding to, Building on or Challenging an answer from someone in their class, they do it in a respectful manner.

Taking it further

When you accept the first answer, can you grade it? 'Thank you, Johnny, that is probably a C-grade answer . . .can anyone add to that to make it a B- or an A-grade answer?'

The awkward interviewer

'I'm not giving up until you give me the answer that I want.'

Keep on pushing and probing your students when they are being questioned. Don't let them get away with weak answers. They'll give you more if you push them more.

We've all seen the awkward interviewer on television. The key to getting great answers is not giving up and being prepared not to accept someone dodging your question.

We all know the students in our class that would rather not put themselves out or go the extra mile to answer our questions. It's our job to push, probe and challenge these students further so they know that we are not going to accept anything less than a well-thought-out and constructed answer every time we ask a question. Students will naturally pause or stop when they think they've given you enough of an answer to please you, so it's important to use your awkward interviewer skills to good effect to keep them talking.

Phrases like this get students to keep talking:

'Hmmm... interesting.'

'Aha... yeah.'

'Keep going.'

Body language can also have a huge effect on our students, enabling them to feel more confident in extending their answers. Let's face it, we all feel far more confident to keep talking in an interview if we get the feeling from the person sat opposite us that they like what we are saying. Try smiling, nodding and using hand gestures to get your students to offer even more in their answers.

Open-ended questions

'There is no right answer.'

Far too many teachers ask far too many closed questions. The talent in highly skilled questioning lies in the ability to get students to think deeply and discuss their thoughts. Closed questions usually lead to short answers that, once the correct answer has been given, close the thought processes of the students.

We all know that students are engaged when they are *doing*, not when they are just being talked at. With this technique, students are actively engaged in regular discussion, having to think deeply about the question because there may not appear to be a straightforward answer. This leads students to question each other's answers, listen carefully to the ideas that their peers have and even begin to actually question the question.

Rather than authenticating answers with a simple 'yes' or 'no', or through encouraging or discouraging body language, responses from the teacher should be 'Why do you think that?' or 'Explain your thought process behind that answer'. This leads to further discussion and explanation from students, demonstrating to everyone that you are creating an ethos in your classroom where discussion is a key element of the learning process.

We also need to remember that this is not an easy technique to just pull out from your sleeve in the middle of the lesson, though. Careful thought and planning are required to strategically craft these hinge questions so that they are constructed and timed to the best effect (see Idea 41).

Teaching tip

Praise your students regularly for the quality of their discussion. Make it clear that we can all pluck a correct answer out of the air from time to time, but that it's the thought process and the discussion that lead to them arriving at the right answer that are to be commended.

Old favourites

'Take complete control of the questioning in your classroom with these old favourites.'

Some questioning ideas have been spoken about in many books before, but still aren't used frequently enough in our classrooms. These two old favourites let you combine many of the smaller questioning ideas previously mentioned in the book into a couple of 'knock out' strategies, which will really make you the king or queen of questioning.

Teaching tip

Why not print the words 'pose', 'pause', 'pounce' and 'bounce' and stick them up at the back of your classroom so that they are always in your line of sight when questioning your students. This way it will serve as a visual reminder throughout the year.

Think, pair, share

Students are far more likely to be confident sharing their views if those views are shared by at least one other person. The 'Think, pair, share' idea is great for groups that are not that confident or forthcoming in sharing their ideas with the rest of the class. Think back to a time when you've been at a quiz and been asked a difficult question that you are not sure of. How confident would you have been shouting your answer out in front of everyone else, without discussing it with anyone first? The same thing applies to our students. They are far happier to share their ideas if at least one other person agrees with them. It creates that safety net where, if they are wrong, they are not on their own.

Once you ask a question, get students to think about the answer first – use your wait time (see Idea 33) and then get students to pair up and discuss their thoughts. After discussion, get pairs to report back to the group with their collaborative answer.

This has the following benefits:

- Students will grow in confidence if someone else has the same thoughts/answer.
- If one student is wrong or does not know

the answer, hopefully their partner can help them out.

- Students have the opportunity to verbalise their thoughts to their partner before being asked to give their answer to the whole class, thus being able to practise what they are about to say.

Pose, pause, pounce and bounce

This is like being a questioning superhero and bringing all of your questioning weapons out in one go! #boom! Being able to put all of your questioning skills together in one strategy is a thing of beauty. To the naked eye it looks like something that just happens and doesn't look that complex, but the trained eye can spot all of the individual strategies complementing each other perfectly beneath the surface.

1 **Pose** your question to the class.
2 **Pause** – use your wait time effectively (see Idea 33) and give the students time to think about their answers.
3 **Pounce** – use your 'no-hands hot seating' strategy (see Idea 34) to pounce on whoever you want. This can be planned beforehand, ensuring you choose the students or groups of students that you want to, or it can be done randomly to add excitement by the use of a random name generator (see Idea 35).
4 **Bounce** – use your ABC of questioning skills (see Idea 36) to bounce answers around the room for students to Add or Build on. Remember to throw in a curve ball every so often and randomly ask the class if they'd like to Challenge that answer.

By putting all of these strategies together in one, you can make this part of your daily repertoire with consummate ease.

Socratic questioning

'I cannot teach anyone anything, I can only make them think.'

If you know how to question students in the right way, by getting them to really think about the topic in hand, then you can start to get them immersed in their learning, taking their engagement to another level. But to do this you need to be ready with scripted responses to their answers.

Using Socratic questioning creates an environment where no student can get away with an answer without being probed for further detail. In a Socratic classroom, questions breed questions and questions lead to conversations, not answers.

There are four types of scripted responses you can use to generate further discussion:

1 The Gadfly – Keep chipping away at them, asking lots of little questions so that the student cannot just offer an answer without a reason or any evidence, e.g. 'What do you mean by that?', 'What evidence is that based on?' and 'Does that always apply?'

2 The Midwife – Give birth to further ideas by asking a question that progresses the student on to thinking about something different or related, e.g. 'How might that affect things?' and 'What made you think of that idea?'

3 The Stingray – Administer a shock every now and again to challenge the conventional thinking of the students, e.g. 'What if the opposite was true?' or 'What would happen if that was not the case?'

4 The Ignoramus – Pretend to have absolutely no knowledge of the answer whatsoever so that the student has to provide a full and detailed explanation, e.g. 'I'm not sure I understand you' and 'Can you break that down for me into simple steps?'

Planning for questioning

'The average teacher asks up to 400 questions a day... that's 70,000 per year or between 2 and 3 million in a career!'

If we ask so many questions and we know it's such an important strategy and technique for assessing knowledge, learning and progress at any given moment, then why don't we spend more time planning these questions to ensure greater impact?

For most teachers, we ask questions 'on the fly' when something happens in our class that triggers our mind into constructing a question that we want students to answer. But how can we be constructing the very best questions to stretch and challenge our students, together with asking them at the optimum point in the lesson, if we are doing this in our head whilst trying to do all of the other things required of us with 30 students in front of us?

When planning a lesson, plan for your key questions that are going to be pivotal in challenging your students and transforming their learning. You may find these questions in your faculty scheme of work or your exam board specification.

When planning questions, think about:

- Who do you want to answer it?
- At what point in your lesson is the optimum time to ask this question?
- How do you want your students to respond to this question – individually, in pairs or in groups (see Idea 39)? Or is it there just to provoke thought?

> **Bonus idea** ★
>
> Plan your questions by using Bloom's taxonomy to ensure that you are stretching your students to use higher-ability thinking skills. For example, rather than just asking your students to describe or outline something, can they analyse or evaluate it?

Question dice

'Roll the dice!'

Getting students to ask the right questions is a skill in itself. By using dice with predetermined styles of questions, you can start to get your students to understand the differences in the type of questions they may ask and actually get them asking them.

Taking it further

You can differentiate your dice quite easily by adding different thinking skills to each dice. You might have one set that includes lower- and middle-order thinking skills and another set that includes middle- and higher-order skills.

I initially saw this technique used with story dice and then with specific foam question blocks, but you can create this technique easily and quickly by either making some bespoke dice or buying some blank ones in shops or online.

The idea is to put the initial of a different higher-order thinking skill from Bloom's taxonomy on each side of your dice. This can be done on card if you create your own, or by writing them onto a blank dice that you've purchased. You'll also need to have a large key visible on your classroom wall, so that the students know that A is for analysis and K is for knowledge, etc.

Once you have your dice, or multiple sets of dice, get your students to roll them when they have a question. Depending on what letter it lands on, the student now has to frame their question to meet that particular thinking skill. Or if your students aren't up to speed with this yet, why not model it for them? Get the students to roll the dice for you, and then ask them the question. The more they are exposed to the different types of questions and the varying complexity of each, the more they will be comfortable answering them on an exam paper.

The hardest question

'You won't be able to answer this one!' Credit to John Pacey, Assistant Headteacher for this idea.

With this technique, you get your students to come up with the hardest possible question they can think of on a specific topic. Students have to go to the very depths of their brain to construct a question that is so challenging that they can outwit their peers.

During your plenary, get students to come up with 'the hardest question' for their partner, who is, in turn, doing the same for them. Let students become competitive and keep scores of points in the back of their books over a period of time. However, make sure that every student who writes a question must also provide a model answer. Creating the hardest question on a certain topic is of no use to the student if they do not know the answer themselves.

Constructing the hardest question also means you always have to be paying attention throughout the lesson, being fully engaged so that you take in the very smallest and most intricate details that other students may miss. This creates complete engagement all of the time, with students constantly looking for opportunities to take on board new learning, especially if it is challenging to others.

This is also a great opportunity to get students to become far more familiar with the higher-order thinking skills that are found at the top of Bloom's taxonomy. Students will soon realise that, if they want to construct a hard question, a question based around the skill of knowledge and application is going to be too easy. They need to start thinking about questions that their peers will be required to analyse and evaluate as part of their answer.

Bonus idea	★

Why not plan a rota, where every student takes it in turn to plan the hardest question for homework so that it can be used as the starter activity for the whole class in the next lesson?

Challenge

Part 6

Timers to increase pace

'Use digital timers to make your tasks accurate and challenging.'

Adding a timer on the board immediately increases the pace and challenge in your classroom, and shows students that you are in charge of the pace.

Getting students to work hard outside of their normal comfort zone is fundamental in great learning. We must push our students further than they ever thought they could go. An easy way of doing this is by setting a time frame for each task that you give your students. However, many teachers fall into the trap of giving students a time frame that they simply do not stick to, giving the impression that the students are in control of the pace, and not the teacher (see Idea 45).

To combat this, ensure that you use a digital timer on your board to show students that you are accurately keeping to the time frame that you have set for any given task. This will push the students to work hard and get them to work outside of their normal comfort zone. It also demonstrates how long they should be working for, rather than just doing the bare minimum inside the first 30 seconds of a four-minute task.

By using a timer on the board, you are clearly in control of the pace, letting your students know how long you are expecting them to work for, and challenging them to finish the task in the set time, rather than the lesson being led by students working in their comfort zones.

Two minutes is too long

'Just hang on two minutes!'

How many times have you said 'I'll be back in two minutes'? Have you really been back to that person in 120 seconds? Or has it been, in many cases, a theoretical two minutes — which, in fact, is probably more like five or ten minutes?

If our brain knows this, and as humans we generally accept that two minutes is not really two minutes, then we need to think very carefully about the messages that we are giving our students in the classroom. Since I started thinking about this a few years ago, I've ensured that I never give students any timed tasks that last either two or five minutes. Instead, I set tasks that last three or six minutes. By actually setting the task for a minute longer, but using a time that they are not used to hearing constantly, the students subconsciously think that it is shorter.

In practice, you can set a group off and say that they have two minutes to complete the task. What you'll see is the class getting on and subconsciously thinking that it will be a theoretical two minutes, which will actually come to an end when they are finished, and not when the clock stops. Try telling the kids that they have exactly three minutes to do the task in and see how they respond differently. This time they know that they are being timed, and they will get working quicker and with more urgency because they perceive the time frame to be shorter.

Teaching tip

It's all in the language we use. As a rule of thumb, stay away from two-, five- or ten-minute activities and instead go for three, six, nine or eleven minutes.

Taking it further

Try combining this approach with Idea 44 to really set the pace and challenge your students to work outside of their comfort zones.

Three-minute motivators

'Get up on your feet!'

Most lessons have a period where it begins to fall into a temporary lull and it's our job to spot this and do something about it to redirect the learning.

We've all been in a class when we were young where we began to get bored. Guess what? That happens in your class every day too... you may just not have spotted it yet! Train your eyes to spot the moments when students start to wander off task. Students are usually engaged at the beginning and towards the end of the lesson, but it's the 20 minutes in the middle of the lesson that can sometimes be the trickiest.

Rather than fighting against this disengagement (especially if it seems to be the whole class), why not shake things up (literally) and get your students out of their seat for a three-minute motivator? The trick is to get them to stop what they are doing, put their pens down and do something completely different for three minutes. You might get them up out of their seat, moving around the class talking to someone else – in fact, anything to get the blood and oxygen pumping around their bodies again so that they are re-energised for learning.

A great example that I have used with many of my classes is Richard Wiseman's 'The Prediction', which you can find on YouTube. Play this video to your students and get them up out of their seats. It's perfect for blowing students' minds for a few minutes before getting back to the task at hand!

The curse of knowledge

'The more you know, the harder it is to explain it to someone for the first time.'

Professor Eric Mazur says that it's often easier for a fellow student to explain a problem or a new piece of learning to another student who is finding it difficult, rather than the teacher.

It is true that the more expertise you have, the harder it is to describe it to a beginner. I'm sure we've all had this experience at some time in our lives before. The frustration of not being able to describe to someone how to do something that seems incredibly simple or easy to us can sometimes be overwhelming.

The reason behind this is that, as experts, we forget the initial problems and misconceptions that people have when learning this new skill. We believe that it is so simple, because we have mastered it, that most other people should be able to understand it and get to grips with it. Unfortunately, it is not that easy. Take, for example, a time when you have had to show one of your parents or grandparents how to use a mobile phone!

The answer is to use fellow new learners to help each other. Once a new learner has just become proficient at a skill, it is far easier for them to teach someone else, or for them to help someone else understand the problem, than for an expert to do it. This new learner still appreciates and understands the barriers and misconceptions that the other learner faces, because he or she has just overcome them.

Simply get students to buddy up or join a small group led by someone who feels they have mastered the skill, and let the new learner become the student coach for a few minutes.

Teaching tip

If students are struggling to grasp key concepts in your class and you have personally tried various methods, don't be afraid to ask for a 'new learner' to help out. Not only will this possibly solve the problem, it will also boost the confidence of students who have been asked to help out and do something that you, as the expert, could not do!

Bonus idea ★

For your own CPD and for more inspiration from Professor Eric Mazur, watch his fantastic Keynote Session at the SSAT National Conference 2012 at www.youtube.com/watch?v=y5qRyf34v3Q.

Competition

'Boys love being competitive.'

Every teacher in every classroom up and down the country will have come across a group of hard-to-motivate, disengaged boys at some stage in their career.

This is not rocket science, but neither is the fact that boys generally thrive on competition. So if you've got a topic that you know is going to be hard to motivate the boys with, why not try to make some aspects of it competitive?

The first thing you need to do is to work out what does it for your boys in terms of rewards, and this will depend on their age. Is it a merit or reward point? Is it a phone call home (see Idea 87) or is it something else? Whatever it is, make those things achievable but competitive. Students love the feeling of 'winning' or 'earning' something, especially if it is something worth having, which they have identified with you. Students can earn points towards these rewards via either your school reward system or a manual system that you use just in your classroom.

If you get a group of really competitive boys, you may also want to limit the amount of rewards that will be given out that lesson, or that week. For example, you might say that you are only going to make two phone calls home, so the two students who score the most points, or work the hardest, will receive this reward.

Taking it further

Boys also like visual competitiveness. If you are going to use a scoring system, make it visual so that the boys can see it and can work towards achieving more points on the board. Remember, you'll also have groups of girls who are equally competitive, so don't forget to try it with them too.

Bonus idea ★

Talk to the students individually and get them to select the reward they are aiming for. Remember that there isn't a one-size-fits-all approach to rewards. Some rewards will motivate some students more than others.

Make it tough

'Nothing worth having in life comes easy.'

Nobody is engaged if a task is too easy. We have to pitch our lessons correctly so that we challenge our students to work hard and so that they feel like they have achieved something at the end of it.

The common mistake that many new teachers make in their first term is that they want to be liked by their students, so they shy away from making their lessons tough and challenging, and instead think that students will like it more if it is easier. That might be fine for the first lesson or so, but your students will soon get bored and feel underchallenged. This then leads to disengagement, poor behaviour and a general lack of interest in your lessons, which is very difficult to pull back from.

Don't apologise for making learning tough. Make it clear from the outset that you have high expectations for your students and that you believe in them. You are going to push them hard because you know they have the potential to do and achieve great things. As students get older and wiser, they will not forgive you if they feel you have sold them short and made things too easy for them.

Use your reward systems to back this up. If you are making the work challenging and the students know that it's going to be tough, ensure you distribute sufficient and relevant rewards to compensate for this.

Bonus idea ★

From time to time, show the students an exam question from a GCSE or A Level (or equivalent) exam paper to really up the challenge. Watch their confidence go through the roof if they can get to grips with it. The next time they meet a particularly difficult challenge in your lesson, they will have more confidence to tackle it.

Teach to the top

'Have we been getting differentiation wrong for too many years?'

Historically, teachers have been taught to almost 'dumb down' subject content so that it makes it easier for lower ability students to understand. Aspirations have been lowered for our less able, and ceilings of achievement placed on them by a distinct lack of opportunity to access the skills and content needed for the higher grades in that subject. We need to rethink our approach to differentiation and start teaching to the top, so that we provide sufficient challenge for everyone.

Teaching tip

Do not use your differentiated resources too quickly with the lower ability students or they will just come to rely on them without thinking for themselves. Keep an eye on all groups of learners in your classroom, especially if it is a mixed ability class, and use your resources when you feel the time is right.

The common mistake that lots of teachers make with differentiation in mixed ability classes is that they pitch their lesson 'down the middle' and then try to differentiate for their weaker students, to ensure that they can keep up with the rest of the class, or provide extension work when their most able students finish the work early or find it too easy.

Although, on paper, this may seem a fairly sensible approach to the non-educated eye, all it serves to do is to not really challenge or support anybody. Our least able students are given lots of resources to make the work easier, and begin to rely on these 'crutches' throughout their learning journey. As for our most able students, they rarely feel challenged and work is usually well within their comfort zone. The 'more of the same' extension work that often comes their way, as the teacher is caught short when they finish so early, does nothing to move them on to the next level or mentally stretch them.

One way of achieving this is by teaching to the top and challenging every student in the group. This is an entirely different model to the one that most teachers have been trained to follow, and aims to support less able students in accessing the higher challenges of learning, rather than catering for the less able first and then thinking of ways to make it more difficult for the more able.

You should start by pitching your lesson to meet the needs of the more able, designing your success criteria in such a way that your higher ability students will be as stretched as the lower ability. Resources, scaffolds and models will then be required for your lower ability students so that they have the tools to help them (when needed) along the way.

This benefits of this approach are:

- Your least able students are given the opportunity to access the entire syllabus. They are involved in all the activities that even your most able students take part in and are encouraged to work hard, with constant modelling of what the top grades look like from the more able in the class.
- These students are also exposed to high standards of literacy, English language and questioning, in just the same way that we are told that students who arrive in the UK with no or little English should be placed in the top groups, because it is here that they are surrounded by the best examples of the English language from which to copy and imitate.
- The most able students in your class are never truly motivated and engaged if they feel that work is too easy or beneath them (see Idea 49). If we are teaching to the top, we are ensuring that our most able students are stretched, challenged and engaged.

> **Bonus idea** ★
>
> Arrange your classroom into groups and have your most able students sit on the table right in the middle of the room. This table will then be the driver of pace and challenge in the class, meaning that you will do more 'teaching to the top' because that is where your automatic focus will be.

Post-it notes for progress

'Write on it, stick it, move it!'

Giving students the ability to assess their own progress can be an incredibly powerful strategy to use in your classroom. Not only do your students have to think about the progress they have made, they can then also visualise it.

Taking it further

Why not combine the use of post-it notes with the Target board (Idea 52) to get students to assess their progress against a set of success criteria? Students can then move their post-it note throughout the lesson whenever they feel they have hit a specific section of the success criteria.

A great way to do this is to use post-it notes. Firstly, they are cheap, cheerful and come in lots of different colours, and secondly, they are movable, giving you progress displays that are easily adaptable and changeable throughout the lesson.

Students can write their name or initials on the post-its, and then use them in the following ways:

- Students write down one thing they have learned during a task or the whole lesson and stick it to a learning wall in your classroom. This way, you can see what students feel they have learned and whether there are any areas that might have been missed.
- Students can write down a question that they still have about the topic or lesson today. These can be stuck to a question wall in your classroom at any time throughout the lesson. You can then review these midway through the session and adjust your lesson accordingly, or at the end of the class to help plan for their next lesson.
- Students stick their post-it note, with their name on, on a continuum line on your board or wall to represent how close they have got to meeting the objectives of the lesson today, or how confident they are with this topic.

Target board

'The odds of hitting your target improve dramatically when you aim at it.' Credit to Jim Smith, Assistant Headteacher, @Jim_Smith for this idea.

Students love being able to aim for a target and hit it. Combining a clear set of success criteria with the ability for students to be able to visualise their progress, and 'hit' certain aspects of it, makes this activity both fun and productive.

Firstly, design a target-style image (like an archery board) on your whiteboard or wall with gold, silver and bronze sections. You can either draw this by hand with marker pens (different colours if you have them) or design it on the computer beforehand (much better for the long term, so you can use it again and again).

Secondly, split your success criteria into three stages – bronze, silver and gold – and display them next to your target.

At various stages throughout your lesson, get your students to go up to the target and place a post-it note with their name on the target in the section that they feel they have achieved. Some students may want to place their post-it note outside the targets if they feel they have not quite achieved the bronze criteria just yet.

Be prepared to let students come up to the board and move their post-it note whenever they feel they have made progress. This way, it will be so much more organic and less contrived by you as the teacher.

Teaching tip

Take a photo of your target board when your students first put their post-it notes on it. Take another one at the end of the lesson to compare the progress. Be sure to show your students, either that lesson or the next lesson, the difference in the two photos and the progress they have all made as a class.

Taking it further

Even if your students don't feel that they can move their post-it note into the next section, why not get them to move it closer as they get more confident with each section of the success criteria? This way, all students can still demonstrate progress, even if they don't move out of a section.

3B B4 Me

'I'm not helping you!'

Far too often, students' first port of call when they are stuck is to raise their hand and ask you. Answering their call for help is all too easy, and all it serves to do is to deskill them. Then, when they enter an examination hall and don't understand the first question, they hit a mind blank because all they have ever been used to doing is putting their hand up.

A simple way to re-engage students in a topic when it becomes hard (rather than looking for the easy way out), is to use the 3B B4 Me technique. This says to students that you will not be prepared to help them unless they've been through the following three sequential steps first:

1 Brain – Have they thought long and hard about the problem before asking you? Have they sat in silence for a few seconds and tried to work the problem out for themselves?

2 Book – Have they consulted their book full of class notes to help them solve the issue? Rereading their own notes might just give them the answer they have been looking for.

3 Buddy – If they still haven't got the answer, have they asked their shoulder partner either side of them? Collaborating and engaging with others can be a great way of solving problems independently of the teacher.

If, after all of the three steps have been taken, the problem has still not been solved, then students can go to the next step:

4 Boss – This is the time that it is perfectly acceptable to ask you, the teacher. The student has been independent in their attempt to find a solution and has not just disengaged at the first sign of challenge.

Let them find their own way

'Getting lost is not a waste of time.'

Lots of things we teach have a direct path to the answer we want, but where is the fun in that? If we only ever allow one path to the right answer, it shows students that all our problems are linear. As we all know, some of the most complex problems in life require a great deal of thinking and discussion, sometimes arriving at the solution via the most surprising of circumstances.

We've all been in a situation where someone tells us a solution to a problem and that their way is either the best way or the only way – remember how motivated you felt. Not very? But now think about a time when you've had to do some serious soul-searching and you finally stumbled upon the solution by yourself. Along the way, you've probably come across dead ends and red herrings, but the ability to stay engaged in finding the solution has finally paid off. You are now going to be far more motivated to look for another solution yourself the next time you are faced with a particularly challenging situation.

By letting students find their own way to a solution, they may also surprise you. The way you see the journey to a solution might be very different to theirs. By opening your mind to the way they think and the way they have arrived at the solution, you just might expand your own mind. Understanding how your students are thinking could even help you to describe the solution to another class. After all, if you can show that you are prepared to learn from your students, they are far more likely to show a growth mindset themselves. Demonstrating your own growth mindset is the best way to be a role model to fellow learners.

> **Bonus idea** ★
>
> From time to time, celebrate and reward the student who has taken the path least trodden in order to arrive at the solution. This way, you are demonstrating that it's more fun to arrive via the scenic route than the express highway.

Digital technology

Part 7

QR code displays

'Help create curious learners who are inquisitive about the world.'

QR codes are so easy to create and use in your classroom. You can link to absolutely anything online, creating displays in your classroom that come to life once scanned. Unleash the power of technology on your walls!

Picture a display board in a classroom. You're probably picturing one that is out of date and boring to look at, with a few pictures about a subject that are barely interesting after the first time you've looked at them.

You can add digital content to these boards by simply creating a QR code that links directly to a website page or piece of digital content. Imagine now being able to have students scan your noticeboards and watch videos of your topic directly on their mobile phones. The possibilities are endless!

All you need to do is:

1 Find a free QR code creator on the Internet.
2 Add the web page of the piece of content you want to link to.
3 Save the QR code image that it creates.
4 Add your QR code to your display.

Creative ways to use QR codes:

- on display boards to make them come to life
- on your classroom door or corridor so that students can scan them whilst waiting to come in
- on the back of toilet doors in your school
- printed on stickers to stick in student books for them to scan at home for homework.

Taking it further

Add QR codes all over your room without any titles or descriptions about what they are for. See how curious and inquisitive your students become. Keep changing the content to keep them fresh.

Bonus idea ★

Create a montage of student work, put it online and then create a QR code that links to it, which is stuck in student books so that parents can scan it from home and see outstanding examples of work from your class this term.

Augmented reality

'Bring your walls to life like Hogwarts!' Credit to Mark Anderson, speaker, consultant, author, trainer, @ICTEvangelist for this idea.

Without doubt, this is one of the coolest inventions I've seen in 'easy to create' technology. This will blow your students' minds when they literally see pictures come to life in your classroom!

There are lots of free apps out there now that enable you to create augmented reality content, and my favourite is Aurasma. Augmented reality is similar to how QR codes work (see Idea 55), in terms of students scanning a certain trigger image, but this time the results are far more impressive! Instead of scanning a code, you scan an image and then the image literally comes to life right in front of your eyes!

The best use of this is where you use the first frame of a video as the trigger image, so that when that image is scanned, the video starts playing right there on the wall. The beauty of augmented reality is that it doesn't open up the video in YouTube or in a web browser – it literally plays like it has come to life on the wall. Very cool indeed!

You can create augmented reality content via Aurasma and a host of various other free websites, and a quick search on the Internet will get you started. Alternatively, you can play around with lots of predesigned content by searching for augmented reality apps that have preloaded content, to see the amazing possibilities that this technology can bring to your classroom. Search the app store for 'Augment', 'String' and 'Inkhunter' to see what's on offer.

Taking it further

Why not create worksheets with hidden trigger images that, when scanned, open up videos of hidden content? Students love the idea of trying to find hidden content, and become even more curious about what might be lurking on the page in front of them!

'Coming soon' trailers

'Coming soon to a classroom near you . . .'

Create short video trailers, like TV adverts or cinema trailers, to whet students' appetite for future topics or lessons. Get them on the edge of their seats in anticipation of what is coming next week!

We all love to know what's coming next in a series or what films are coming out this summer. It's only natural to be curious about what you are going to see or do next. Yet how many times do we create this feeling for students in our classrooms? How many times do you dangle the carrot in front of them by showing them what is coming up in the next few lessons?

All it can take is an image or poster that you have created about the next lesson or topic, which you can flash up at the end of the lesson – maybe even when the students are packing up and are standing waiting for the bell to go. Or maybe you are a bit of a whizz with technology and you want to create a brief video clip or a series of photos put together with music to showcase what the students will be doing next? Imagine the buzz that this might create in your lessons when students are already looking forward to an upcoming topic that might be a couple of weeks away.

Either way, you will begin to get your students excited about what is coming up and get them looking forward to their learning, rather than just turning up to your classroom.

Text your answer

'See your answer hit the screen.'

You can now poll your students and have their answers pop up on your interactive whiteboard within seconds of them answering your question on their smartphones. A great way to gain instant feedback from your students.

Due to the advances in technology, you no longer need to buy expensive hand-held quiz answer pads to enable students to participate in quick-fire quiz questions that generate their answers on your board. There are now many websites that do this for free, together with analysing your results in graphical form and informing the students whether they are wrong or right. My favourite sites for this are Poll Everywhere and Socrative.

Using these sites can be extremely fun and engaging for any students who have a competitive nature lurking inside them (see Idea 48). The Socrative website even scores points for correct answers and generates leader boards to increase the competitive element in your classroom.

If you do not want to use it for competitive quizzing, you can use Poll Everywhere for students to text what they have learned, or even as a response to a group activity or classroom task where they have to text in an answer to a problem.

Students usually find this engaging if it is used every now and again to spice things up, rather than every lesson. Like anything else, if the students engage in it and find it fun, you usually find that you get more 'buy-in' and better responses to your questioning.

Teaching tip

Be aware that, unless you are enabling the students to use the school Wi-Fi, the students might have to pay for each message they send, depending on their mobile phone price plan. You also need to have an alternative way to answer the questions for students who do not have a smartphone. Read Idea 61 for tips on how to manage students using their phones in class.

Taking it further

Most of these websites and services let you build a profanity list of words that you don't want to hit your screen. There will always be one student who tries to ruin your lesson with a word that you certainly don't want to see broadcast to the whole class!

Death by PowerPoint

'Please, Sir, not another PowerPoint!'

Most teachers' go-to presentation method is PowerPoint. So imagine the diet of presentation material our students get, lesson after lesson. They are potentially exposed to five hours of PowerPoint per day, every day.

Teaching tip

Trying out new software is not something I'd advise doing the night before a lesson. Set yourself some time aside at a weekend or during a holiday to learn how to use it and get fairly accomplished with it before you unleash it on your class!

Although PowerPoint is quick, easy and can be made to look very corporate to suit your school requirements, there are many other ways to present your lesson material to your students. Now I'm not suggesting we all throw PowerPoint out with the bath water – far from it – but by doing something different every now and again, it can get students to sit up straight in their seats and engage in something a little bit different from the norm.

My three favourite alternatives to PowerPoint are:

1 Prezi.com – Prezi is an online presentation website that allows you to create a canvas that you can move around and zoom in on. However, be careful – too much zooming, moving and rotating can leave your students feeling seasick!

2 Sway – Sway is Microsoft's new alternative to PowerPoint, which allows you to create professional-looking presentations that look great on any device in minutes. It also allows for interactive content to be included in your presentations, making it much more engaging.

3 PowToon.com – PowToon is an online video-creator that lets you create animated videos and presentations using either predefined templates and characters or a more bespoke method, depending on your levels of creativity and expertise.

Whichever you choose to use, the opportunity to step away from the norm and mix up your delivery is one that you should try.

Toon your classroom

'A picture paints a thousand words.'

Cartoons and comics are a great way of getting students to engage in your subject content by combining pictures and key information in an easy-to-digest format. With this idea, you can easily create stunning-looking revision resources that students can store in their image gallery on their phone.

Creating professional-looking, comic-style images on the Internet is now free and easier than ever before. The best way to do this is to search for a free cartoon- or comic-maker website on the Internet. My favourite websites for this are Comic Life and Toon Do.

My advice would be to create a one-sided revision comic for a topic that you want your students to learn. The comic should include images relevant to the topic, plus all the key messages in a sequential order, similar to a comic telling a story. Once created, you can save these comics as images that you can either use digitally or print for your classroom.

In my experience, the most effective use of 'revision toons' has been when my students have downloaded the JPEG images from our school VLE directly onto their phones. The beauty of this is that students can then store them in their photo album for independent study, any time and anywhere. This is particularly useful in the run up to exams, so that students always have a bank of easy-to-read revision toons, from which they can quickly digest the key points, wherever they are and whatever they're doing.

Taking it further

Why not get students to create their own revision toons on a list of set topics for an upcoming exam? If students create their own, they are more likely to take ownership of them, and the content and key messages will sink in quicker.

Bonus idea ★

Once students have created their own revision toons, get them to submit them to you so that you can choose the best ones to be used by the whole class. If students know that theirs may be chosen for the class set, they are likely to put more effort in.

BYOD

'Bring Your Own Device.'

So many teachers complain about the lack of quality ICT access in their subject, but we sometimes forget that the majority of students come to school with technology in their pockets, which is more powerful and adaptable than the computers on our desks. Take advantage of this technology and be ready to unleash new learning opportunities.

In most secondary classrooms now, if you have 30 students sat in front of you, you can pretty much guarantee that each of these students will have a smartphone in their pocket or bag, which means you have access to 30 computers without leaving your classroom. As long as your school doesn't still ban the use of mobile phones, even for learning purposes, it's something to consider.

Providing you can control how students use them, and that you are strong enough to tell students when they can use them and when they can't, then why wouldn't you want to utilise this technology?

Potential uses (apart from specific apps):

- stopwatch
- calculator
- torch
- camera / video camera / slow motion camera
- voice recorder
- note-taking device
- compass
- web browser.

And those are just the native apps that are preinstalled on most smartphones!

Digital leaders

'Use the digital natives to train the digital dinosaurs.'

Use tech-savvy students as digital leaders to train staff on creative and innovative uses of technology in the classroom. These leaders can be 'booked' by staff so that they can get up to speed with the latest uses of technology.

Most schools have student leadership positions that centre around head boy/girl, prefect duties and, in some schools, sports leaders. But increasingly, schools are now starting to develop their very own digital leader positions and capitalise on the significant digital skill sets that our digital natives have.

You've probably witnessed this before and it may be the case in your school now: some of the students know far more about the technology they are using than the teachers. In schools where digital leaders are recruited, these students are on hand to help showcase new technologies to teachers, provide staff training and facilitate the growth of new technologies into classrooms across the school.

Potential uses of digital leaders by staff:

- Deliver CPD-style training on new apps and technology to groups of staff or even the whole staff.
- Deliver one-to-one sessions (on demand) for staff who are struggling with a certain piece of technology.
- Provide advice and guidance for staff who are looking for some inspiration on the use of technology to spice up a certain aspect of their scheme of work.

Imagine the engagement levels of students in your school if they know they could have the opportunity to teach their teachers!

Taking it further

Create a digital leader team that you recruit for every academic year. Students have to apply via any creative digital medium they see fit. Have the digital leader team meet like the school council do, so that they can lead initiatives, bring new ideas to the table and drive the use of new technologies in your school.

Skype an expert

'We can't be a world-class expert on everything we teach.'

Wouldn't it be amazing to get a leading expert in the subject or topic you are teaching to teach your students for free? Now you can with Skype; you just need to open your mind to the possibilities of who!

As we all know, we are forever charged with providing a world-class education to our students, but with the increased level of content and the diverse range of skills we need to cover, it is virtually impossible to be an expert in everything. What could be more inspiring than having a world-class speaker talk to your students and extend the level of expertise that you can provide?

The beauty of Skype is that it is free and you probably already know how to use it. It also breaks down all the barriers that you normally face when trying to bring in an external speaker, such as time, cost, distance, etc.

Take a look at the 'Skype in the Classroom' websites for a huge selection of leading organisations all over the world who are waiting to Skype into your classroom and inspire your students. There are organisations and speakers split into countries, subjects and age groups, who have specific experiences and skill sets that they would love to share with your students. All you then need to do is contact them, set up a mutually agreeable time and bingo, you're ready to go!

Connect your classroom to the world

'Where there is teamwork and collaboration, wonderful things can happen.'

Wouldn't it be great to connect your class to another class, either in this country or across the world, to collaborate on a learning project together? It's like having a class penfriend, but far more exciting!

The best way to get your classroom connected to the world is to join the thousands of teachers who are already signed up to the 'Skype in the Classroom' website. Here you can submit a request to connect with a class in a defined country or age group, or for a specific project/ syllabus topic. Alternatively, if you're looking for inspiration, you can browse the thousands of requests already posted and connect with a classroom that interests you. Once you've contacted the teacher and talked it over, you simply swap Skype IDs and hook up at the agreed time with your classes – it couldn't be easier!

The potential for this type of learning project is huge. You could work collaboratively on a project that both classrooms are studying, or you could even use the expertise that the other class already has to teach your class. Imagine a situation where the students in your class had to learn something (potentially about something from British history, or about your local culture or heritage) so that they could teach it to another class on the other side of the world who needed to learn about it.

When the audience is real and other people are relying on you, the motivation to do your very best goes through the roof!

Taking it further

Surely it's a no-brainer for MFL teachers to hook their class up to schools in Europe for authentic speaking lessons? And for geography teachers, wouldn't it be great to get students from another part of the world to teach your students what it's like to live in different climates?

Bonus idea ★

Why not sign up and submit a request on the 'Skype in the Classroom' site or post a request on Twitter to look for a class from a certain country or part of the country to join you for a collaboration project? There could be a teacher out there looking to do the same thing!

Take a virtual field trip

'Give your students a window to the world in your classroom.'

Take your class on an inspirational field trip without having to leave the comfort of your classroom. No more risk assessments, cover requests and financial barriers to compete with!

We all know how much red tape there is for taking students out of school for a field trip. The paperwork and time it takes to organise usually puts you off to begin with. Then there is the financial element. Either your school has to foot the bill or you risk making it prohibitive to lots of families. All that is just for a trip within your own area – imagine the look you'd get from your head teacher or business manager if you went with a request to take your class to the Amazon rainforest!

With Skype, you can now make these trips of a lifetime possible. Take a look at the 'Skype in the Classroom' website for organisations across the world that would love to Skype in and take your students on a special guided tour of their part of the world. Imagine the buzz that this would create if your class were going on a virtual field trip to a part of the world they'd never even dreamed of going to!

This doesn't have to be a truly global visit, though. You may even be able to get your class to visit the shop floor of a factory in your own town via Skype. Opportunities like this make visits that might not have been possible, due to health and safety restrictions, possible. Certainly, it's a great way to bring a careers lesson to life.

'How to' guides

'Anytime, anywhere learning.'

In the digital world we live in, the learning style of many teenagers has been moulded by watching 'how to' guides, gameplay 'walk throughs' and product reviews on YouTube. These short digital guides give step-by-step instructions, complete with visual guides, to help us better understand a concept. So how can we tap into this and use them in our classrooms?

If we know that this is how our students are engaged in informal learning outside of our classrooms, then we'd be stupid not to try to utilise the power of the digital 'how to' guide. Students are very used to this style of modern learning and, for large numbers of our students, they will tell you that this is how they prefer to learn. These digital guides can be great for skills that are sequential, demonstrating them in a step-by-step process that is very easy to follow.

Similar to the flipped learning approach, but this time within your classroom, students can learn at their own pace, pausing the video to write notes or to practise the skill, rewinding the video to go back to certain points they might not have understood the first time around, and returning to the video during the lesson when they require some extra help or support, independently from the teacher.

Not only does this help teach the skill well, it also creates a very focused and independent climate in your classroom. Distractions become almost eradicated because, with their earphones in and their focus on their screen, they are completely engaged and immersed in their learning.

Flipped learning

Part 8

Flip your classroom

'Delivering content is the easy part; the expertise comes in working with students to fulfil their potential.' Credit to Jon Bergmann, Flipped Learning Pioneer, @jonbergmann for this idea.

Reorder the way you deliver your lessons, away from the traditional approach, enabling students to obtain the main content of the lesson at home, before they even enter your classroom! Homework now becomes watching a short video, leaving time in the lesson to do what they would have normally done at home without your support.

Teaching tip

Plan for what you are going to do for the students who don't watch the video. Have some textbooks or reading material ready for them so they can take notes and quickly catch up on the content that they should have watched for homework.

What if your students had watched a video at home that you had prepared, containing all of the new content that you wanted to share with them?

Typically, a flipped class will start with a plenary-type activity, which aims to assess the understanding that the students have gained from the homework video task. The teacher can then assess whether the class are ready to move forward. During this activity, the teacher or other students can address any misconceptions that students may have about the topic. Once the teacher is happy to proceed, the class will move on to a more challenging task, which asks the students to use their new learning and apply it to a deeper learning activity. This may be an extended writing task, a project, a presentation or anything where the students have to assimilate their learning and put it into context.

Throughout this task, the teacher will go from student to student, speaking to them about their work and providing individual support and progress checks.

Taking it further

Try to keep your videos to no more than ten minutes in length for older students and even less for younger ones. Bite-size chunks are far more likely to be watched and are more engaging.

- Create a screencast, video or narrated PowerPoint of the content you want to deliver, and make it available to your students via either your school's internal VLE or a public video-sharing platform like YouTube.

- A great way to produce these videos is by using the free Microsoft Office plugin for PowerPoint called 'Office Mix' or, if you prefer using a tablet, look for the superb 'Explain Everything' app in the app store.
- The extended writing task or assessment, which they would have done for homework, can now be done in the classroom in an environment much more suited to learning.

Letting students learn new content at home, in their own time, can have the following benefits:

- Own pace – Not everyone in our classroom learns at the same pace. Students learning this content in their own time and at their own pace, is a far more enjoyable experience for them.
- Stop, pause, rewind – Maybe a student didn't quite catch what we said, or they need to hear it again to process what it really means. In a flipped environment, this is easy. Simply pause, rewind or stop the video as many times as you want.
- Time to think – When somebody is talking to you and giving you new information, it is very hard for your brain to stop and think about it. Being able to pause the content and think about it is really important. This enables us to process the learning, make connections with our previous learning and then move on more confidently.
- No peer pressure to pretend to understand – In a flipped environment, it does not matter how long it takes someone to understand something. They can revisit the video or article as many times as they want. They can refer to a textbook, ask a friend or family member, or even do some further independent research until they get it.

Bonus idea ★

Tell your students to bring their phones and a set of earphones to your lesson. If they feel they need some help or support, tell them to be independent and rewatch the part of the video that they need to without the need to disturb anyone else.

Pre-reading

'Knowledge is power!'

One of the biggest misconceptions about flipped learning is that it has to be about watching a video. Although this is probably a more engaging way to deliver the new content at home, it doesn't have to be that way. Finding a great article or extract for the students to read can be just as effective.

Due to advances in modern technology, lots of teachers are turning to videos to help them deliver flipped learning, but using carefully chosen articles for students to read is just as important.

A great way to make your lessons authentic and up to date is to search for and select a recent article from either a traditional newspaper or an online website that is talking about your topic within a real-world context. Take a copy of the article and make it available, either digitally via your VLE or go 'old skool' and photocopy it for each one of your students.

The benefits of providing a pre-reading source prior to your lesson are:

- Students are encouraged to read more than they are normally used to.
- Students have to take notes on what they have read, encouraging the good note-taking skills that are essential for exam success.
- You are providing real-life examples where your topic or subject is relevant.

To ensure that your students have read the pre-reading homework, ask them to get their notes out when they arrive in your class and then start with a question-based plenary activity.

Students create the content

'You can be the expert.'

We don't always have to be the expert in the room. Why not hand over some of the responsibility to your students? Getting them to create the content of the videos can be a really good way of engaging them further in their learning.

Sometimes, even though we are supposed to be the experts, it's very difficult to get what we think is a relatively simple concept through to our students (Idea 47). In these cases, our students can sometimes do a better job than us because they know the misconceptions that their peers are facing, as they too have faced them. So what better way to combat this than getting the students to produce their own short flipped learning video for a designated topic?

If you draw up a rota, where each student (or pair of students) is given a topic that they need to research and then produce a short introductory video for, you are suddenly going to get videos for every single topic you are going to teach that year. Once you've got the videos and you are happy that they are accurate and meet the requirements that you set out, they can be used as the flipped learning content that your students need to watch every week.

By creating their own videos, your students will not only have to know that topic inside out, but they'll also be able to show off their ICT film-making skills, as well as their communication skills. By letting your students be creative in how they present their designated topic, you're bound to be amazed by some students in your class who you never thought would get that involved in a piece of homework like this!

Bonus idea ★
Make it competitive. Make all the videos public to the class once they are produced and then get students to watch them and try to create a better version of someone else's. They'll start to really look at the content, like an examiner checking for key content that has either been missed out or not clearly explained.

Recycled revision remix

'Don't reinvent the wheel.'

If you've followed the previous two or three tips, then you may already have a bank of videos introducing and exploring all the content on your syllabus. You've now got all you need to create 'any time, anywhere' access to revision for your students.

Giving 24/7 access to your digital revision materials is part of 21st-century learning. If your students can learn and revise when and where they want to, at a touch of a button, and without having to give it more than a second's thought, then they are going to be far more engaged in their learning. You might also find that, because students have had access to these videos all year long, they are already ahead of the game in their revision!

But with any revision-based activity, the less engaged students will always tell you that it's boring, because 'We've already done this, Sir!' So you may have to come up with some ways to recycle and remix your videos so that they stay fresh for your students as they begin their revision.

- Create specific playlists that contain only the relevant videos for a certain topic. This way, students are directed to exactly the right content and don't spend time hunting around for it, or wasting time watching the wrong videos.
- Remix two or three short videos into a lone one by using a simple Moviemaker-style programme that lets you add multiple clips together to make one longer clip.
- Add new bonus content at the end of some of the clips so that students are more interested in rewatching old videos.

Lights, camera, action

'Capture the magic in your classroom.'

A great way of introducing a topic, or generating curiosity and excitement for an upcoming unit, is to watch a short clip of a practical element of the lesson that has been filmed. This works brilliantly in subjects such as science, technology, music, drama and PE, but could be equally effective in more academic subjects if you can think outside of the box.

Students will normally tell you that the practical element in any lesson is usually the most fun and engaging. Imagine the excitement and anticipation by starting the lesson off showing the class a very short clip of the experiment they are about to undertake, or a clip of students taking their food out of the oven or grinding some metal on the angle grinder? By filming students taking part in these activities throughout the year, you can create a bank of clips to use for all of your classes and different year groups.

Although the primary purpose might be to engage and excite, these short video clips can also be used for help and guidance. Practical elements are also sometimes the most complex parts to our lessons, and many of your students could probably do with a little guidance prior to attempting them. By watching a brief video clip of the practical as a whole, or a specific stage of the practical, it will increase their confidence to give it a go when they might have been apprehensive about their ability to be successful.

Once you've got a bank of video clips, they can be used as part of the flipped learning process for students to watch at home before they step foot into your classroom, meaning you can get onto the exciting stuff faster!

Teaching tip

Whenever your students are taking part in practical activities, grab your tablet, camera or digital device and capture some footage. Create folders on your hard drive for various practicals and then just dump it all in there.

Flipped mastery

'I'm not stopping until I've mastered it.'

This sense of intrinsic desire to master a subject or topic is a far more powerful motivator than purely to achieve a good grade or impress friends, family and teachers.

Once the flipped learning approach has been developed in your classroom (see earlier ideas on flipped learning) and your students are comfortable with this approach, you can endeavour to set out on a mastery approach to learning. In this style of teaching, everyone starts from the same point at the start of a topic or course, but they progress through at their own pace once they have mastered the current level, topic or task.

A mastery approach requires a set of standards to be achieved at the end of every topic, and only when you feel a student has mastered that set of standards, to either your required level or their potential, can they move on to the next topic.

This engages students in their learning in the following ways:

- Students do not get disengaged waiting for other students to catch them up. Once they are ready and they have mastered a certain topic, they can move on.
- The harder they work and the quicker they master the topics, the sooner they can move on to new and more interesting topics.
- Using the terminology of mastery demonstrates the highest possible expectations in your classroom.
- When students have been told that they have mastered a certain topic, it gives them great confidence when tackling even the most challenging tasks, and answering future exam questions.

Active learning

Part 9

Project-based learning

'Get them engaged, keep them engaged.'

Primary school students love working on topic-centred projects, yet we seem to forget this at secondary school. By immersing them in a whole project centred around a topic, you can grab their imagination, and then keep them engaged via an extended process of asking questions, finding resources and applying their knowledge.

Take a look at your syllabus. How many different topics/units do your students have to know? Wouldn't it be easier and more memorable for them if you could reduce this down to one per half term, rather than one per week? By concentrating on an overarching theme for the project, you can include multiple, smaller topics that all feed into the main theme.

If you ask your students to just finish something off for homework, or you only give them 20 minutes to produce something, they will assume that it can't be that important, and therefore the effort they put in will be minimal. However, tell them that this project will run over multiple lessons and that their end product or report will take them a few weeks, and you demonstrate that this is more than just a finishing-off exercise.

If you want to set up an effective project-based learning activity, you should look to involve the following:

- Students learning and then using their knowledge to tackle realistic, real-life problems.
- Students having increased control over their learning.
- Students working in pairs or groups.
- Teachers serving as facilitators of inquiry and reflection rather than as the experts.

The Apprentice

'You're fired!'

This is project-based learning with a competitive twist, based on the famous TV show fronted by Lord Sugar. Teams in your class will battle it out to win half-termly challenges that require independence, teamwork and application of knowledge.

So you've done project-based learning before and are looking for something a little bit different... look no further! Split your class into four groups and give each group a team name, just like on *The Apprentice*. These are the teams that they will work in for the next few weeks, battling it out against the other teams in your classroom for supremacy.

Your job as Lord Sugar is to carefully plan a project-based task that has multiple assessment opportunities, roles and tasks, and that lets your students demonstrate their knowledge of a unit of work on your syllabus. Once you've written up the task brief, build up the hype by having it ready in an envelope for each team to open the next time they enter the class. From there on in, you are just there as an advisor and as a judge. The teams need to be independent in how they go about their business and how they choose to execute the task.

Remember that the final piece of work that they submit or present is only a fraction of what this task is about, so a very effective way of groups demonstrating their trials, tribulations, thought processes and successes is by getting them to continually write a digital blog. This way, they can add photos, videos and daily summaries of their work to demonstrate their group progress. You can easily create free blogs on either your own school VLE or on sites such as Blogger, Wordpress and Weebly.

Teaching tip

Get the class to watch a few clips of *The Apprentice* so that they get the general idea of what they are about to do, and how effective teamwork is essential if they want to be successful.

Taking it further

Can you get a local businessperson or an associate of the school to be the real business judge at the end of the process? Each team would then have to present their idea or final product to the judging panel, just as in the boardroom on *The Apprentice!*

Teamwork makes the dream work

'Individually we are one drop; together we are an ocean.'

Let students engage in collaboration by encouraging structured group-work activities, but with designated roles that students must undertake. By carefully planning these roles, you can ensure that everyone is crucial to the overall success of the group task.

Teaching tip

Some students may take to certain roles better than others and may gravitate towards them. However, in order to develop well-rounded students who get to practise all of these roles and skills, ensure that groups rotate roles regularly.

One of the classroom activities that less experienced teachers usually shy away from is collaborative group-work activities. It can be seen as a way to hide for some students, by letting stronger characters take the lead, making it very difficult to assess how much work each individual has done and how much credit they can take for the overall output.

When planning, ensure that you plan your group members based on the desired outcome you are looking for. For example, don't just naturally assume that splitting up all of your five really confident and strong characters into one in every group will be a good thing. All that will probably happen is that they will dominate and lead each group. Now, you might want this... but, on the other hand, you might want other, quieter students to step into the limelight.

Roles such as group manager, equipment manager, reporter and photographer can easily be planned for in most classroom-based group tasks, without much creative thought. You can then score groups each lesson on how each of their members has performed. For example, did the equipment manager have all the equipment and resources out ready for the group to work? Was everything packed away neat and tidy? Scores can then be generated and filtered into the ongoing assessment of the groups' work.

House of Commons

'Intellectuals can debate, idiots just argue!'

Develop your students' debating skills by giving them the opportunity to think deeply and to have their voices heard in structured debates. These debates can be centred around topical areas of your syllabus and, if carefully chosen, can promote thought, challenge and intellectual discussion.

To be able to see both sides of an argument and debate your point thoughtfully and respectfully is something that not everyone can do straight away, but it can be taught.

There will be lots of topics in your subject that are sure to fire up strong feelings in your class amongst your students but we sometimes forget to exploit and explore these true feelings that they have. When students use their feelings in their learning, they start to make deeper learning connections and are far more likely to be able to recall this information later.

Tips for structuring a great classroom debate:

- Set up your classroom like the House of Commons, with one half of the room facing the other half.
- Split your class into two equal groups.
- Write the title of the debate, the hot topic or the question on the board.
- Tell one half of the room they are debating for the argument, and the other side that they are debating against it.
- Use some sort of object, such as a water bottle or teddy, as the microphone. Only the person holding it can speak.

Teaching tip

Establish a set of 'house rules' that everyone must abide by. For example, everyone must be silent whilst the speaker speaks, raise your hand if you want to speak, no interrupting and no laughing at or mocking of other people's points.

Taking it further

It is usually far harder to argue a point that you personally don't believe in. Use this as a way of challenging your more able students, by placing them on the other side of the argument to the one they naturally believe in.

Choice and ownership

'Take charge of your own learning.'

Give students the choice on how they present their evidence to show that they have understood and learned a topic. Far too often we stipulate the medium by which a class have to show they have understood the lesson. But why? Surely we just have to evidence that they have learned it?

Not everyone likes doing PowerPoint presentations. Ask any student what they are bored of after a year at school and they'll probably tell you that it's just that. So why do we stipulate how our students demonstrate their knowledge?

Rather than stipulating the medium by which your whole class should evidence their learning, why not give them the choice? By opening up the choice of medium they can use, you are suddenly getting them to pick the one they like best, therefore immediately increasing their engagement in the task. After all, the reason you have set them a task is so that you can assess their knowledge, not so that you can judge how well they can design a PowerPoint presentation!

Tips for giving students choice:

- Create a list of popular mediums that they can pick from.
- Make sure that the same students don't keep picking the same medium throughout the year.

Students will surprise you with the effort they will put in, once they have the choice of medium. You will be amazed to find out that students have hidden artistic, film-making and media skills that you knew nothing about!

Takeaway homework

'You choose!' #TakeAwayHwk inspired by Ross Morrison McGill, @TeacherToolkit.

Let your students choose how they present their homework by choosing from a menu of tasks or activities so that they can take more ownership of their learning and show you their creative sides.

If students are enjoying what they do and have creative licence to present their knowledge in a slightly different way to normal, you'll almost always find far more time and effort spent on the task.

Think about all the different ways that students can present their homework. Once you've listed them all down, think about the level of difficulty that each one carries – this way you can probably split that list into three sub-sections: starters, main courses and desserts (main courses being the harder tasks and starters and desserts taking less time or effort).

You might also want to differentiate within each sub-section by applying a tariff or pricing structure to show which tasks are more difficult and will therefore earn more rewards from you if completed to a high standard.

Now get creative and make your menu look great so that it engages your students. You might want to come up with your own classroom design, use the corporate school logo or something a little similar to some of the more well-known high street restaurants and fast food outlets.

Now every time you set a homework task, get students to pick a meal or a combination of meals from the menu.

Teaching tip

Tell students that they have to spend a certain amount of money in your restaurant every term. This way it stops those lazy students just picking the starters every time!

Taking it further

Get your menus printed and laminated and then stick them in cheap, 'stand up' photograph holders that you can buy from places like Ikea, to make them look even more like menus on the table.

Bonus idea ★

Create an order form in the back of students' books that students keep adding to every time they choose a menu item, so that you can keep track of how much they have spent and which tasks they have chosen.

Fresh air fix

'Sometimes all you need is a bout of fresh air.'

Why not move the learning outside every once in a while? Not only will the change of scenery be a surprise and probably a welcome change to your students, but the fresh air will also help stimulate their brains.

Teaching tip

Make sure you stress to your students that your classroom rules still apply. Just because you are outside of your classroom doesn't mean to say that all rules are off!

As previously mentioned in Room layout (Idea 3), students can get bored of the same seat, same room, same time of the day every week. Suddenly telling your students that you are going outside today can immediately lift the mood of even the most disengaged of classes!

Although you might let the students believe it's on a bit of a whim, make sure you have thought this through before you jump in head first without being able to get back out! Always check that:

- The weather is not going to ruin the learning (too cold, wet or windy and you've got no chance of getting students to listen and concentrate).
- You are not disturbing another class by being outside.
- You have planned a good space that is conducive to the type of learning you are hoping will take place.
- You have cleared it with your head of department or senior leader so that they know where you are going to be in case of emergency and that they are happy for it to happen.
- You've planned enough time to get your class back to your classroom and packed away so that they can get to their next lesson on time.

Take a walk around your school site and look for ideal spaces for outdoor learning.

Bonus idea ★

Due to the nature of outside spaces and the extra space you may have, this might be a great opportunity for you to go outside with another class and do more collaborative work.

Public audience

Part 10

Pride wall

'Be proud of their achievements with you.'

Cover your walls with the amazing work of your students and they will know how proud you are of their work. They'll also want to put that extra effort in if they know it's going to be displayed on your wall for other students to see.

We collect so much work from students every year, but how much of it is used as a model for other students to see the standard that you require? With modern advances in technology, this now doesn't just have to be in the form of a written piece of work. This can now be a photo of a practical activity or even a link via a QR code (see Idea 55) to a video of a student making a product or taking part in a performance or presentation.

Not only are you using these pieces of work as a model of excellence for students in other classes or other year groups further down the school, but it also serves to act as motivation for students. No matter what front some students put on, or whether they tell you otherwise, the fact that their teacher wants to put their work on the wall of their classroom, for other students and staff to see, has to be a nice feeling for anyone.

Calling it your 'pride wall' gives it even more merit, showing students how proud you are of the time and effort they have put into producing their amazing work. You can then also distinguish this wall from any of your other classrooms walls, on which you might have posters or signs. Only the best work gets to go on your pride wall!

Gallery critique

'Growth is a result of listening to constructive criticism.'

Instead of you being the only judge of how well a piece of work has been undertaken, why not open it up to the class so that they all become judges of each other's work?

Far too often we see the students' finished products as the end of the learning process but, in reality, this is where the real learning should start to take place. Once everyone has finished their work, it is the ideal opportunity for the class to step back and maturely view everyone else's work.

Rules:

- All criticism must be constructive and mature.
- Nobody is allowed to pass comment without backing it up with evidence or accurate justification.
- All students must understand the exact success criteria of the task before critiquing.

Performing a gallery critique, where students have to comment on other students' work against a set criteria, develops the following:

- students who can judge the quality of a piece of work against a set criteria
- complete understanding of the criteria necessary to be successful
- students who can start to pick up good ideas from each other
- sharing of outstanding practice
- students who can see the standards that are expected across the class.

Taking it further

Get the students to come up with their own rules on how they should critique each other in order to receive the most effective feedback possible.

Bonus idea ★

Allow a set time for each student to view a piece of work before they can move on. This way, every student is looking at a piece of work individually with their own thoughts, rather than crowding around one piece and being swayed by other people's opinions.

Public pride

'Use the eyes of the local community.'

Why not ask for a display space in a local community building to showcase the amazing talents of the students in your class? Not only will it be a great way to motivate your students, but it will also serve to publicise your school.

Teaching tip

When displaying work, ensure that the work is clearly marked with the student's name and age/year group, together with the topic or task that it is related to, so that the public can see exactly what the student had been asked to do. This way, they can put into context how good the piece of work is.

This is another way to motivate your students by displaying their very best work that you are proud of. However, in this instance, changing the location of the display from the walls of your classroom to a public space can make all the difference. Think about the businesses that you have connections with in your local community – could they give you a space to display some of your best work for the community to see?

Imagine being told by your teacher that he or she was so proud of the piece of homework that you'd done that it was going to be on show in the local community for everyone to see – a space in the local library, the foyer of the local leisure centre or even the local supermarket! How often do young people get the opportunity to have their work displayed for members of their family and their friends to see?

Bonus idea ★

One of the best ways to display student work is by holding an annual art exhibition. A gallery-style display of the very best artwork from your art students will look beautiful and will certainly turn a few heads in one of the local businesses in your community.

Think also about the promotional aspect that the school would gain from this – members of the community stopping to see the amazing high standards that you are setting in your classroom and the quality of work that students from your school are producing. What better way to showcase your school, but with authentic pieces of work from students instead of the usual quotes from Ofsted that always get touted about.

Go social, go global

'The eyes of the world are watching.'

With modern technology, we can now showcase the talents of our students to the world in only a few clicks. By using popular social media channels like Facebook, Twitter and Instagram, we can promote their best work to a global audience, direct from the classroom, only a few seconds after a piece of work has been finished.

If you still think that merit marks and stamps in books are the biggest reward you can give a student, then you need to wake up to the new digital age. The currency that the digital natives are now using is 'likes', 'hits' and 'views'. If you can showcase the work of your class via a school or faculty social media page, students can be motivated by this very currency.

As a piece of work, a photograph or a video is posted, the students can see in real time how many people have liked it, shared it or even commented upon it. This real-time feedback is far more motivating than anything you could write in red pen. This is 'real' and from 'real people'. Not only that, but the ability for their work to be seen in minutes by their family and friends is something that was never possible when it was just stuck up on the wall in the classroom.

Proud parents can now share the post, retweet it and forward it to a wider audience, instantly creating a snowball effect. From a piece of work carefully crafted in a student's bedroom, it has become a digital masterpiece, seen by hundreds – and maybe thousands – of people across the world.

Teaching tip

Have a camera or mobile device available in your classroom at all times to capture a great piece of work, so you can upload it there and then. It will blow students' minds when they see that it's already had likes from across the world only minutes after they have finished it!

Taking it further

At the start of the year, promote your social media channels to your students. Ask them to get their phones out and follow it.

Bonus idea ★

Think about setting up multiple social network channels to reach a wider audence. You can also link these accounts, so that you only have to post something on one channel and it will send it to another, therefore saving you time.

Class blogging

'An audience of one is not that motivating.' Credit to David Mitchell, @DeputyMitchell for this idea.

Forming a class or a faculty blog is a great way of not only showcasing the very best work from your students, but also getting students to think about the audience they are writing for and the publishing skills they need to communicate with different audiences.

Teaching tip

There are lots of free blog sites out there for schools and teachers to access that require little or no previous experience to set up. Take a look at sites like Blogger, Wordpress and Edublogs to get started.

In the same way as using social media sites (see Idea 83), blogging can significantly motivate your students because their work is going out to a real audience. However, this time, the intent to write for and publish to an external audience is there from the beginning. In this case, the best student work is not chosen to be typed up on the blog; students know from the offset that's where it's headed, so the motivation is there from the start.

The student clearly knows that what he or she is writing will be published online via the class blog. The student must then understand the audience of the blog so that they can use their communication skills to effectively engage with that audience. Knowing that your work will be available to be read by the public only a few seconds after it is published can be a huge motivator for everyone.

Taking it further

Try to make blogging a regular feature of your class. If there is regular and up-to-date content on your class blog, parents and the wider public are more likely to be interested and may start to visit your blog without being prompted to check for new articles.

There may be areas of your curriculum with significant links to the local community that your students can blog about. These articles can then be easily shared with members of the community, the wider public and even the press, via a simple email link. Knowing that your writing will have an impact on the local community and that members of the public will be interested in your work will be sure to increase the motivation levels of your students.

Guest critique

'Feedback from the real world.'

Sometimes students don't see teachers as real people, so when they get feedback from someone from the 'real world', it can potentially increase its significance. By getting members of the public to be guest critics of your student work, this can add that little more spice to a potentially dry topic.

The most effective way to do this is by using a class blog (see Idea 84). Students publish their work to the blog so that it's available for people to read outside of the school. You can then arrange it so that members of the public are able to provide feedback on your students' work.

There are a couple of ways to do this:

- Allow comments in your blog settings so that anybody can comment on any article to generate comments from parents and other students who have read the post and who can provide some constructive feedback.
- Approach some key individuals in the local community and ask them if they'd like to be part of a guest critique team for your class blog. With this idea, you would alternate between your team of guest critics so that they do not feel overloaded with work. Asking someone to look through a few posts every once in a while shouldn't be too much trouble.

Getting external people involved in the critique process can really help your students and the school. Firstly, it gives your students that authentic feedback that they are looking for. Secondly, it's another way of engaging the local community and key individuals in the success of your students, thus promoting the great work that you are doing in the school.

Taking it further

Why not approach leaders of local businesses who are influential players in the local community? Once they get on board, they are sure to spread the word through the local area about what they are doing, generating extra publicity via word of mouth.

Praise and rewards   **Part 11**

Unconditional respect

'Everyone wants to try hard for someone who really respects them.'

The foundation that engagement and motivation are based on is having someone who respects you unconditionally. Without this, materialistic rewards and extrinsic motivators only go so far. But if you know you've got someone who is always there for you, no matter what, then you'll always work hard to please them and make them proud of you.

Every day is a new day in your classroom, and students should be greeted at the door (see Idea 12) with unconditional respect. You are the professional in this relationship and you should always be modelling this behaviour to your students. Showing your class that you believe in them goes a long way. The reason they have achieved so much in your class might be down to the relationship you have with them and the fact that they know you'll never give up on them.

However, the minute that student detects that your respect is now conditional, or that they have lost your respect, then their engagement levels will drop dramatically. Why would they bother giving you their best anymore if they perceive that you have started to give up on them? Some students don't have the resilience to win your respect back or even know how to go about doing this, so the easiest thing to do is to disengage.

Starting each lesson as a new day with unconditional respect for everyone is essential in gaining complete engagement from your students. Don't let anyone think they don't matter because they've fallen out with you. We're adults and we're professionals; we're trained to love and respect each and every one of our students.

Friday phone calls

'Happy weekend!'

Every parent loves to receive a positive phone call from their son or daughter's teacher, but imagine the extra impact it might have on that family if it was received on a Friday afternoon, right before the weekend!

Positive phone calls home are something we all should do more of. The impact that a two-minute phone call home has can be monumental. The problem is, we usually run out of time in our normal week and these 'nice' tasks get put to the bottom of our pile more often than not. However, if you value the importance of such a call and the impact it can make on a student and their family, then you might want to start putting it higher up your priority list.

The key here is the timing of the call. By setting aside 30 minutes before you go home on a Friday, you can probably make ten to 15 quick calls to some of your hardest working students that week, to tell their mum or dad how proud you have been of them and that their hard work has not gone unnoticed. As a parent, receiving that call right before the weekend will simply make your Saturday and Sunday so much better, as you beam with pride all weekend!

Students will also start to really value the timing of the calls because, the chances are, they will be spoilt or subject to a treat over the weekend! They'll soon all be clamouring to be on your Friday phone call list!

Teaching tip

Don't always just call your best students. Think about using some of these calls to build relationships with some of your hardest-to-reach students. Catch them doing something great during the week and then surprise them with a lovely phone call home.

Postcard on the fridge

'Wish you were here!' Credit to Paul Dix, @pivotalpaul for this idea.

We all like to receive a postcard through the letterbox, but what if it was a postcard from your son or daughter's school, celebrating a great piece of work they have done or congratulating them on a brilliant test score? Most of us would give this pride of place . . . on the fridge!

The postcard home not only does the obvious, in congratulating the student and highlighting his or her great news to the whole family, but it also communicates it to anyone else that walks in the house.

This serves two purposes. Firstly, the more people that see the postcard and comment on it to the student in question, the greater their sense of achievement for what they have done, hopefully leading to a sustained increase in engagement in your class. Secondly, it's a great advert for your school for all of these people to see that the school – and you as a teacher – really values rewarding students, sharing their great news with their family. Who wouldn't want to send their students to a school like that?

Tips to make it happen:

- Get your faculty/department or school to get some postcards professionally printed with the school corporate branding included on the card.
- Set yourself a goal to write ten postcards home per week to begin with.
- Write a quick, handwritten 'well done' note on each card.
- Drop them into the school office on Friday for them to be posted.

Note in the book

'Make it personal.'

A lot of schools now have grand reward programmes, spending thousands of pounds each year on amazing rewards for their students. However, we sometimes forget that the personal touch from a teacher, in the form of a written note in students' books, is sometimes the best motivating factor of all . . .and it doesn't cost you a penny.

Although whole-school reward programmes are great, and lots of students are motivated by the many amazing and shiny rewards that are on offer, the one thing they do lack is the personal touch. Students may pick up reward points from teachers all over the school and then 'cash in' their reward points for a gift from the reward store at the end of term. The problem is, this becomes very impersonal and it's never handed out to the students by the members of staff that the students have picked up reward points from.

There is still, and will always be, a place for a quick written note in a student's book, telling them how well they have done and how proud you are of them. Not only is this personal from you to them, but it is also private and immediate. Some students struggle with accepting rewards in front of others and feel embarrassed, so it becomes easier to not achieve than to have to walk to the front of assembly and collect their reward. Being immediate, this also directly links to the piece of work they have done, so they can see the connection between what they have done and how they have been praised. In the alternative method of rewarding students at the end of the term, you might find that some of them struggle to remember any concrete examples of work to justify their reward.

Taking it further

Some students won't show their parents their exercise books, so why not take a picture of the page you have written on, together with any work they have done to justify this written praise, and email it or use your school's texting-to-parents service to send it home.

Surprise visit

'Surprise, surprise!'

Written notes, reward points and phone calls are all great personal rewards from a teacher to a student, but nothing is more personal than a special visit from a teacher when you are least expecting it.

This might not be the easiest or quickest of rewards, but it might be one of the best for building strong relationships with some of your harder-to-reach students. What it entails is setting aside half an hour in your week when you are not teaching to go and visit some of your students in another class. You might have highlighted these students when you have been marking their work during the week.

Use the half an hour you have set aside to find where they are and then you can go and surprise them by knocking on their classroom door and asking the member of staff if you can chat to them outside for a minute. A quick conversation with the student to tell them how impressed you have been with them will go a million miles. Hearing it come out of your mouth, rather than just reading it, will make all the difference.

Students have a very perceptive radar for staff who do that little bit extra for their students and they will soon start to really appreciate you taking the extra time out of your day to do this for them. By going that extra mile, they are bound to pay you back in bucketloads in your lessons.

Digital badges

'Collectors don't stop until they've got a full collection.'

Collecting badges has been part of your upbringing if you've ever been a Cub Scout or Girl Guide. The sense of pride and achievement you get when you've been working towards a badge and you are finally presented with it is immeasurable for some. Now, with digital technology, we can make this cool.

Most of you may now be familiar with digital badges in your life. We can be rewarded digitally with a badge congratulating us for anything from walking the required steps in one day, to completing a professional development online course. The reward is immediate, it's visible and it's most likely shareable on your social media networks if you choose to do so.

This can easily be built into your classroom praise-and-reward routines by using online digital badge platforms, such as Class Badges, Open Badges and Credly, to design and issue your badges to your students. You might set up a hierarchy of badges that students have to work towards. Students might have to complete a certain number of homework tasks, pass certain aspects of your course or achieve something even more creative. Remember, the focus here isn't the actual reward, it's the working towards it.

If students don't know what they are working towards and can't visualise it, then the reward that comes out of the blue hasn't motivated them. It's just made them feel good after the event. The trick here is to use these badges to motivate your students to work hard and get their badges before their peers do. A bit of healthy competition never hurt anyone!

> **Bonus idea** ★
>
> Make a colourful wall display, showing all of your digital badges and what students have to do in order to claim them. This way, students can see what is on offer and what they have to do throughout the year in order to complete their collection.

Support your local team

'Fancy going to see United on Saturday?'

Finding a reward to effectively engage and motivate some of your harder-to-reach boys can be tricky. However, there is one thing that usually floats the boat of many of the boys in your school — football. Imagine the ability to reward groups of students with free football tickets to your local club every week!

Schools have tried to motivate students with certificates, stamps, sweets and prize draws, but most schools fail to find the holy grail of motivational tools. Although football isn't going to motivate everyone, it has a big pull for many of our students and this naturally includes boys, the group that most schools need to motivate the most. Using football tickets as a reward for good behaviour and effort might just be the ticket you've been looking for.

The good news is that most football clubs will probably be happy to offer schools discounts, especially if you are wanting to buy tickets in bulk. You might even want to consider buying a set amount of season tickets for the school so that you have the ability to reward students every time there is a home game (at certain points of the season, this can be twice per week).

The trick here is not just to buy child tickets, but to also buy a couple of adult tickets as well. Having staff take students to the match (maybe the year leader of the year group that is attending) enables high-quality relationships to be developed away from the school building in a less formal setting. Students really appreciate this and, just like the PE teacher who takes students to fixtures and competitions, students start to see you going the extra mile for them.

Praise effort, not achievement

'It's not about perfect, it's about effort.'

If we constantly praise attainment in our classrooms, then it creates a culture where the most intelligent will always come out on top. This can be demotivating for many students, who, even if they try their hardest, will never reach the heights of the most able.

Instead of praising attainment, start praising the amount of effort that has been put into a piece of work; you can create a far more inclusive culture. Everyone can now feel like it's a level playing field and that they can be rewarded based on what they put in, not what they produce.

A rewards strategy like this has two main benefits:

1 Firstly, you begin to look at how hard your students have tried. The gifted student who has produced an A* piece of work may have only had to put in a fraction of the effort that a student who has been struggling this year and has just managed to get a C grade has.
2 Secondly, it shows students that hard work is recognised. The highly intelligent, coasting students, who are just doing enough to hit their high targets, are suddenly getting less praise than everyone else. If they are motivated by praise, they'll soon work out that they need to be demonstrating more effort in their work to get noticed.

One thing students always say is that they want teachers to be fair and consistent. What could be fairer than a system based on the amount of effort students are willing to give? If you try hard, you'll be rewarded – a simple message that, if you can engrain it into your students, will pay dividends for them as they go through life.

Taking it further

Praising effort rather than attainment links into the popular 'growth mindset' theory by Professor Carol Dweck. In this theory, every person has the ability to grow and develop their skills, irrespective of their starting point, but it's all about having an open mindset to believe it.

Assessment and feedback

Part 12

Regular progress checks

'I'm doing just fine.'

Help students stay on track and engaged by providing regular opportunities for progress checkpoints so that they can monitor their own progress. Like anything we do in life, if you can see you are making visible progress towards your goal, you are far more likely to be motivated to continue, irrespective of how hard it is.

Taking it further

Once students have mastered the ability to measure their own progress, get them to start peer assessing. This way, they can not only see how well they are doing, but they can also start to look at their partner's work through the eyes of a teacher or examiner.

If we can get into the habit of separating our lessons into more bite-sized chunks of learning (see Idea 31), then this naturally lends itself to the opportunity to provide students with regular chances to monitor their own progress against a clear set of criteria. The more you do this, the better the students will become at being able to maturely and accurately rate their own progress.

To make your progress checks effective, there are two main ways to conduct them:

1 Students assess their progress against a clear set of assessment criteria. The criteria are provided before the task begins so that students know what is expected from them. Students can then use a tick list or a RAG-rated colour scale to see whether they have met the individual elements of the criteria, or how far they have got in meeting them.
2 Students are provided with a list of tasks or sections of larger tasks that have to be completed within individual bite-sized chunks of time. This helps students to keep on track throughout a lesson. If they keep up with what has been expected in each time chunk, they know that they are going to be on track to finish the task in the desired time.

By making it easy for students to be aware of how well they are doing, you will make it easy for them to stay engaged in their learning.

Feedback, not marking

'I listened to your advice and it worked.'

We all know that feedback is one of the most powerful interventions that we can use as teachers, but how motivating is it? If you can engage your students via your written feedback in their books, you can motivate them to constantly want to do better, seeking to improve their work as a result of your carefully chosen words.

High-quality feedback is needed to engage the student into acting upon the words that you write, so that they can improve their work further. If you can get this right, your feedback can be a huge source of motivation and engagement to your students.

Tips for ensuring that your feedback engages your students in wanting to improve their work:

- Use their name. Once you use somebody's name, the words instantly become personal.
- Try to pick out some positives from the work so that you do not come across like you are just picking at faults.
- Identify some key areas that you feel that the student could do better. Be explicit in how they might have done this better. Providing an example may help some students.
- Set the student a quick task to demonstrate that they can improve this part of their work. This gives the student an opportunity to practise this straight away, rather than having to wait a few weeks before they get the chance again.

No longer will students see your feedback as just a judgemental statement, but instead they will look forward to reading your comments because they will be a source of advice and motivation to constantly improve.

Bonus idea ★

Try taking away the grades on your feedback and just provide comments. Lots of students just look for the mark or grade and don't pay enough attention to the written comments. Watch how much more attentive to the comments they become when you remove the grade.

Pre-assessment

'Let's see what you know before we start.' Credit to Sarah Ledger, Assistant Headteacher, Teaching and Learning, @sledgerledger for this idea.

Getting students to assess their own knowledge and skills before they start a new topic is becoming more and more common in classrooms up and down the country. Letting students see their own starting point on a topic gives them far more ownership of their own learning and, in turn, engages them in their learning journey.

A simple way of doing this is to provide an assessment task or test at the beginning of every topic. This is very easy to set up and administer, and it provides the following information to the teacher:

- You know exactly what students do or don't know, meaning that you can create the right levels of challenge for that group.
- You can avoid disengaging your students by repeating skills and content that they have already covered and are already competent in.
- Different students may have significantly different starting points, meaning that your differentiation strategies might need to be creative and innovative.

There are also significant benefits to the students from the pre-assessment:

- Students gain confidence from doing well on a pre-assessment activity. The fact that they already know a little bit about a new topic may suggest to them that they might do quite well over the next few weeks.
- Having seen their starting point, via the pre-assessment, it is very easy to see how far they have come once the topic ends and a post-assessment activity takes place. Confidence levels significantly increase if they can visibly see how much progress they have made from the start of the topic to the end.

Let them set their own goals

'Take responsibility for your own learning.'

We don't always have to be in charge of the learning goals. Give students the opportunity to set their own goals and you'll be surprised how accurate they can be and how it makes them think about where they are and where they need to get to.

Students are used to being given targets for everything they do in school, from maths to behaviour to attendance, but have you ever stopped to ask your students whether they agreed with those targets, or whether they even understand where they have come from? We have all probably experienced a target-setting culture, where the targets don't mean anything to us because we have no idea how somebody has come up with them in the first place. The target may seem unattainable or, quite frankly, just ridiculous.

By including your students in the ownership of their individual goals, you are giving them the opportunity to become much more responsible and reflective and, in turn, far more engaged in their learning. If you give your students the chance to reflect on their own performance from time to time, and then ask them to come up with what they need to work on or do better in their next piece of work, you might just be surprised at how accurate and perceptive your students are.

Once your students get into the habit of doing this, you'll find far more motivation to meet their targets, because that's exactly what they are – THEIR targets, and not someone else's. Suddenly, you start to see reflection, ownership and purpose in their work. It also becomes far easier to hold them to account, because you are holding them to their targets, not yours.

Taking it further

If you are concerned that your students might not challenge themselves sufficiently with their own targets, why not check them all over before you sign them off? This way, the student gets to construct it, but you can cast an eye over it to ensure that it meets the needs of their true potential.

Traffic lights

'Are you good to go, or do you need to slow down?'

Understanding the progress your students are making throughout the lesson is essential in helping you drive the pace and challenge. With traffic lights, students can very quickly and easily assess their own understanding and progress, but without having to shout it out to everyone else in the room.

When delivering new content or ideas, we usually rely on questioning to dynamically assess the knowledge and understanding in the classroom. However, this seldom involves everyone. Quite often, answers can be taken from a range of students and it's assumed this is a representation of everyone in the classroom. This can be quite misleading and also requires constant questioning and interruptions in the learning from the teacher.

With traffic lights, students are encouraged to engage in their own self-assessment and quietly demonstrate this to the teacher. This can be at any point in the lesson, with students simply displaying their red, amber or green card on the front of their desk. The teacher can then see which students are struggling, need more time or are flying, just by looking around the room. This is far easier for the less confident students and creates a much 'safer' environment for students to express their struggles and triumphs.

My tips for using traffic lights:

- Create a class set of small, laminated traffic light cards.
- The cards can either be individual cards or a set of three on a key ring loop, so the cards can be simply flipped over to the desired colour.

Chin your boards

'Show me what you got!' Credit to Danielle Bartram, Lead Practitioner, @MissBsResources for this idea.

Getting all students engaged in your questioning and dynamic assessment can be a challenge. However, with the use of mini whiteboards, everyone can take part. This way, every question can be an opportunity to get students engaged in deep thinking and for them to demonstrate their thinking to you.

What if every subject had mini whiteboards and pens out on desks as part of their daily equipment available to use? The ability to engage far more students in your questioning and assessment is key to keeping students on task mentally throughout the lesson. Knowing that at any minute the whole class is going to be asked to think deeply, and then share their answer with the whole class, ensures that even the hardest-to-reach students stay engaged.

The term 'chin your boards' refers to students having to hold up their boards with their answers on, just below their chin. This way, everyone gets the opportunity to answer. The benefits are as follows:

- All students are engaged in every question, having to think deeply more frequently.
- Students know that all of their thoughts and answers are being taken on board by the teacher.
- The teacher is able to assess the knowledge, understanding and progress from all students.
- Students are able (if the teacher wants it to happen) to turn around and see what everyone else has answered, thus adding self-confidence if a significant proportion agree with them, or helping them to see where they may have gone wrong if it is the opposite.

Teaching tip

Although the mini whiteboards may be a cheap purchase initially, keep an eye on the amount of whiteboard pens you use. These have a habit of 'walking', so it would be good practice to do a quick check at the end of every lesson before anyone leaves that the equipment is still on the desk ready to use for the next class.

Digital feedback

'I don't know what you mean, Sir!'

It's very difficult to find the perfect way to write a piece of feedback so that the student knows exactly how you felt about it. Our words can be taken out of context and sometimes completely understood. The ability to sit down and talk it over with a student one to one would be so much more effective if we only had the time — and with digital technology, we now can.

Choosing to record your verbal feedback, instead of writing it down, can give the student a better insight into what you actually mean, and not just what they have read into your words.

The benefits of providing such feedback are that:

- Students can pause, rewind, fast forward and watch the video again.
- You can highlight the area of work that you are commenting on, whilst talking about it.

With advances in modern technology, this has never been easier to do. If you want to get started with digital feedback, here are my tips:

- The easiest way to begin is just by recording your voice whilst you are filming over a piece of work. You can use your fingers to point to the words or paragraphs that you are referring to.
- Use an app such as 'Explain Everything' to import the student work, then add a voiceover, together with arrows, circles and highlighter lines, to show the student exactly what you are talking about.
- Upload your video file to your school VLE as an individual digital feedback file for each student.